Collecting
Household Linens

Frances Johnson

77 Lower Valley Road, Atglen, PA 19310

to Judy Johnson

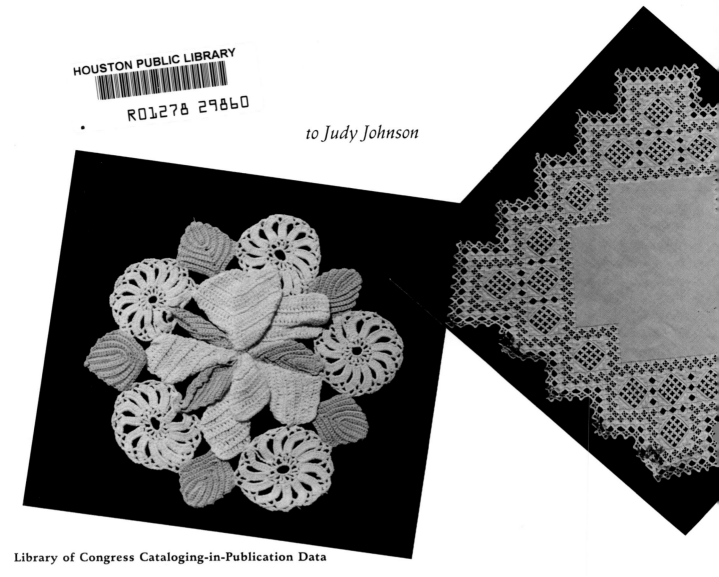

Library of Congress Cataloging-in-Publication Data

Collecting household linens / Frances Johnson.
    p.   cm.
ISBN 0-7643-0111-X (paper)
1. Household linens--Collectors and collecting--
Catalogs.
I. Title
NK8904.J646   1997
746'.075--dc20   96-34007
                                        CIP

Copyright © 1997 by Frances Johnson

Printed in China
ISBN: 0-7643-0111-X

Designed by "Sue"

Published by Schiffer Publishing, Ltd.
77 Lower Valley Road
Atglen, PA 19310
Phone: (610) 593-1777
Fax: (610) 593-2002

Please write for a free catalog.
This book may be purchased from the publisher.
Please include $2.95 for shipping.
Try your bookstore first.

We are interested in hearing from
authors with book ideas on related subjects.

Contents

Portion of Peruvian-woven blanket showing the work and the design. Blanket
$250-$350.

Chapter 1
Fabric, Homemade

Today there is such a wide variety of fabrics available in the stores that no one gives a thought to where and when weaving first began. There was a time when weaving fabrics for both clothing and household linens was a major chore. Not only did the housewife have to weave it, she had to prepare raw materials for both the spinning and weaving. In most cases it was a year-long chore.

Weaving began so long ago that its origins remain a mystery, and it is doubtful after all these centuries anything will ever be found. Although there are no authentic records, it is believed that weaving developed long before looms of any kind. Most researchers agree the idea of weaving probably originated with the weaving of weirs many, many centuries ago. The weirs were needed to catch more fish to supplement food supplies. It was soon discovered that the more closely the weirs were woven, the more fish one could catch. This gave the fishers the idea for making other things to be used around the house, such as mats and baskets. To add a little beauty to the otherwise drab baskets, they began making dyes from familiar things like herbs, roots, plants, and tree barks. Later it was found that these same dyes worked well on home woven fabrics. It is also believed the first weaving of cloth or fabric was done by staking long cords, maybe small ropes, on the ground, and then weaving the yarn back and forth through them. Some of the Indians of South America, especially the Peruvians, still weave beautiful fabric without a loom. They simply take a couple of branches, one for the top and the other for the bottom, wind yarn over both (they are very skilled at the task), then they weave more yarn back and forth through it. They

make their own yarn from the wool obtained from the llama, alpaca, and vicuna. As late as 1986 one Peruvian family was weaving fabric that way to make the Poncho-type coats they were selling at an Indian Reservation in the Everglades. They did their weaving there so the buyers could see how the coats were made.

Whether or not the Navajos are still weaving on branch frames, often referred to as off-loom weaving, is unknown, but it is known that as late as half a century or so ago they were making some of the finest blankets, and making them on branch frames. They became famous for their blankets, both bed size and saddle blankets. Much of their income through those early years was derived from the sale of their blankets. Their early sales had been of the barter variety as they traded their blankets to other tribes for whatever they made. But as white families moved into the area to start settling the West their cash sales increased.

The Native Americans weren't the only ones to barter or sell their wool. It is known that from around 1850 on the Shakers sold or bartered their excess wool to other Shaker communities, and maybe even to the public. They always kept large herds of sheep, anywhere from 1,200 to 1,500 at each community in the early days. Today there is only one Shaker community left, Sabbathday Lake in Maine—and they are still raising sheep, dying, and spinning their wool to sell to anyone who wants to use it in their knitting.

Wool yarn was probably the first made and used when weaving began, as it was readily available and in most cases plentiful. The men generally sheared the sheep while in most instances the women did the rest of the wool chores including washing, dyeing, carding, spinning, and weaving it, although there are quite a few records of men doing all the latter chores as well. Preparing the wool for spinning and weaving was a long, drawn-out process, but probably not as dull as the repetitious chore of spinning or weaving. When preparing the wool there was the washing which was necessary to remove the oil and dirt from the wool. Then there was the carding which was done with wool cards—two paddle-type tools with wire teeth set in leather that sort of combed the wool. It straightened and aligned the fibers so they would spin into smooth, even skeins of yarn. The wool could be carded which would produce a woolen yarn, or it could be combed, a process that produced a worsted yarn. Another tool, the wool comb, was created to handle this chore.

Dyeing the wool wasn't a difficult chore, as most of the homes at that time and for centuries later had a dye pot full of indigo on the hearth. Now the spinning and weaving could become monotonous, but the ingenious spirit of our ancestors soon devised ways and means of making the chores fun. Most of the spinners were young girls, and reports are they took their spinning wheels to the park or town square where they had contests to see who could spin their wool the fastest. They could visit with each other, or they might prefer to spend the time learning to spell or maybe memorizing the multiplication tables. The spinners could learn anything that didn't require the use of their hands as they had to keep their hands free to keep the spinning wheel humming. Spinning was so easy and so repetitious that one didn't have to think about it, just do it. And spin they did, because in those days they figured it took eight spinners, working full time, to keep one weaver supplied with yarn. This also explains why every female member of the family was taught to spin at an early age; her yarn was needed to supply the mother and older girls who graduated to weaving as they grew to maturity.

Slowly but surely, new labor saving devices were being invented and patented such as the spinning jenny that doubled the production in carding in the factories. It was invented in 1764 by an English engineer, but it would be years before it was widely used. A man named Kay invented a fly shuttle during this time and another named Bell invented cylinder rollers. Then in 1794 Eli Whitney of Westboro, Massachusetts, patented his cotton gin. It was designed to separated the seed from the cotton. One of the early models of his gin is in a restoration in Westville, Georgia. Upon examination one soon re-

alizes it didn't separate a lot of seed from the cotton at one time—in other words it was a slow process. But it was so much better than the old method used previously when the entire family gathered at night to pick the seeds out of the cotton. Even after the invention and widespread use of the cotton gin, people living in the middle and northern states where cotton was grown on a very small scale, just enough to fill the quilts they would make that winter, still picked the seeds out by hand. Then in 1804 Joseph Marie Jacquard designed punch cards to be used in making designs in woven coverlets, now called Jacquard coverlets. But none of these inventions had much effect on the majority of people, as they just didn't have the money to buy the new factory-woven fabric. They were accustomed to growing, preparing, and weaving their own fabric, so they continued to do just that. They also continued to weave their coverlets as they always had using wool yarn dyed with native dyes and woven in old familiar patterns that had been passed down from one generation to the next.

Growing and preparing flax for making linen was the most difficult task in fabric making and it required the longest period of time. Flax was planted in the spring and harvested in late summer or fall. After it was cut, the seeds were removed to be saved for the next planting, and it was placed in a stream, usually a rather strong flowing stream as the rotting flax could make still water stagnant and foul-smelling. This rotting process was also known as retting in some areas. With the rotting or retting completed, the flax stalks were put in the flax break or brake. The style of the break varied as they were handmade, but they were all large, heavy and awkward to use. One seen recently was made of a medium-sized log, one about 12 to 15 inches in diameter. A section of the log had been cut out, removed, and then fastened back with a handle that could be raised for the flax to be inserted and then the piece brought back down. The weight alone was enough to "brake" or crush the softened husk or shell, leaving the desirable linen fibers intact. The next step was to pull the unharmed fibers through another handmade tool, the hetchel or hackle. Both names were used, but hackle was more popular in the mountain areas where spinning and weaving were practiced until the middle of the present century. The long fibers that came out of the hackle were used to make fine linen thread while the short, tough fibers called tow or toe were used to make thread for weaving heavy fabric that would be used to make sacks or some types of work clothes. By the middle of the nineteenth century, wool yarn, linen, and cotton thread could be bought already prepared, or if the weaver preferred, they could send their own wool, flax, or cotton to one of the many factories to be prepared according to their specifications. But this cost money, something so many of the weavers didn't have. They were also accustomed to preparing their own yarn and thread at no cost and weren't about to spend money on something they could do themselves.

All these chores have brought us a wealth of antique tools that not only introduce us to the ways our ancestors lived, but are very sought after as antiques so many people use to decorate their homes, especially the newly-restored keeping rooms. Not everyone uses them for decoration. There are many people who became involved in the "back-to-the-land" movement a decade or two ago. They didn't collect the fabric making tools just for pleasure, but actually to use as our ancestors used them. There are still a large number of people spinning and weaving today. Regardless of why they buy them, there are few collectors who can resist buying at least one or two of the old fabric-making tools. Since lots of spinning and weaving was being done, especially in the mountain areas, as late as the 1950s many people still remember fabric being made in their grandparents' homes.

And we must not forget silk although little, if any, was ever spun and woven on the home looms in this country. Silkworms were brought to America because it was felt they would thrive here as the climate seemed perfect and there were plenty of mulberry trees. Unfortunately, the plan didn't work out and the Colonists soon abandoned the project. But the story of the discovery of silk is so fascinating it bears repeating briefly.

The history of silk goes back to around 1700 when the fourteen year old princess Sing Li Chi, wife of Emperor Hoang-ti, discovered through a long period of trials and errors how to successfully unwind the cocoons. It wasn't long after that they discovered how to weave the thread. For her success in unwinding the cocoons, Sing Li Chi from that time on was referred to as the "Goddess of the Silkworm."

For a century or so China was able to guard her secret of unwinding the cocoons. Finally, the secret leaked out and Japan, according to legend, was very jealous. When the Japanese were unable to get information any other way, they sent two priests to China who were able to hide some silkworm eggs in the staff of their canes and smuggle them back to Japan. Soon Japan was making silk as fine as that made in China. They became so proficient that by the first of this century they were producing about 60 percent of the world's raw silk supply. In fact, about this time the demand for silk became so great they could no longer supply the demand with the one harvest per year. They solved this problem by having three harvest per year—one in May and June, another in July and August, and the last one in September and October. Like all the other threads, silk could be mixed to form another type fabric.

Like all other endeavors spinning has its legends and stories. Perhaps the best one is about the English lady who in 1745 spun a pound of wool into 84,000 yards of thread, or 48 miles. As we all know there is always someone waiting to beat any record, and this supposedly happened in the thread spinning category. Shortly after the English lady set what she hoped would be a record, someone else reported spinning a pound of wool into 115 miles of thread. We have to remember that there is a lot of wool in a pound; it is very light in weight, and if spun into very fine thread, it would go a long way.

Silk thread doesn't seem to be a big seller today probably because so few people now do needlework. But it must have been big business for a few decades before and after the turn of the present century. It seems that silk thread was used in much of the knitting, crochet, and embroidery that was being done then. As proof of that an undated catalog from the Eureka Silk Manufacturing Company with offices in Boston, New York, Chicago, and St. Louis has been found. It appears to date around 1890. Silk thread must have been very popular as they offered twenty one varieties, everything from embroidery and saddler's silk to French etching silk.

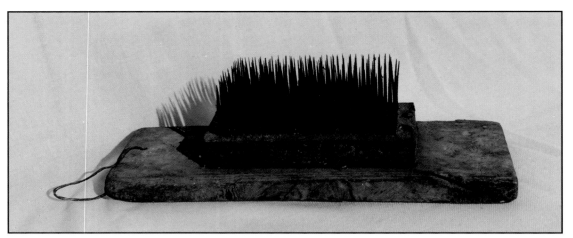

The flax hatchel or hackle was one of the first tools needed in preparing the flax for spinning. $100-$150.

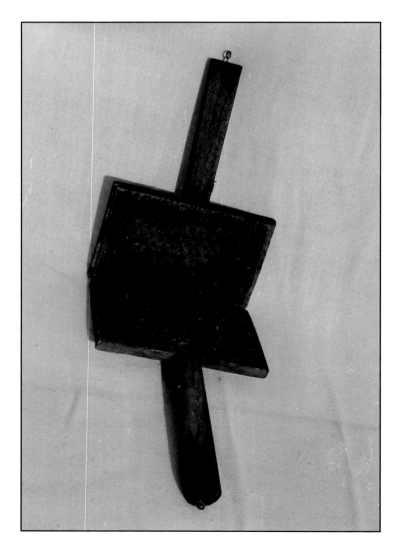

The wool comb was necessary in preparing wool for spinning. They are old, rather scarce, and not too sought after today, but prices have remained strong due, no doubt, to their age and scarcity. $85-$100.

Wool cards were necessary in preparing the wool for spinning. $20-$30 per pair.

Cotton cards were equally as important in preparing cotton for spinning. $20-$30.

The drop spindle is one of the older tools in spinning yarn. $65-$95.

This flax wheel sold at auction recently for $150.

Flax wheels were made in a variety of styles. Since they are smaller than the yarn spinning wheel, they are more collect-ible today by those who only want them for decoration. $150-$200.

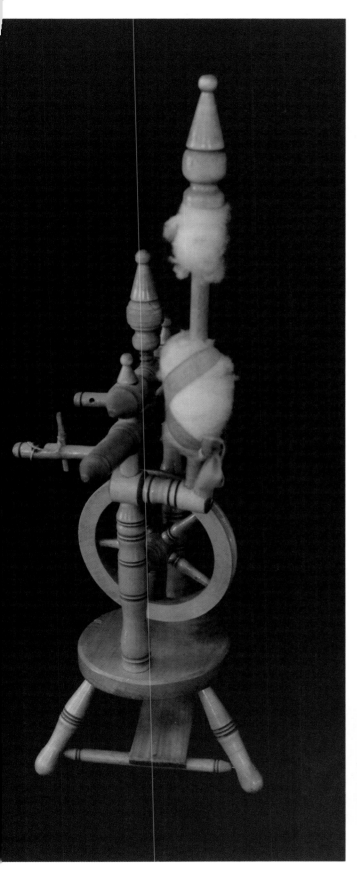

Miniature flax wheel was probably made as a novelty. $25-$35.

Once the yarn or thread had been spun it was often wound on a squirrel cage swift. $100-$175.

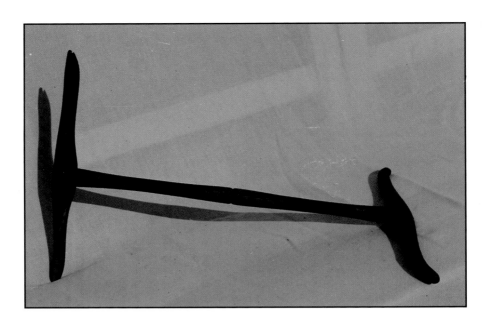

A niddy noddy was also used to wind yarn. $45-$75.

Small loom often called a hand loom. Was used to weave fabric for small items. $40-$55.

This umbrella swift is not one of the earliest but is very attractive. $50-$85.

A quiller and scarne winder, probably from Canada. Crank on wheel axle is missing. Scarne bobbins were slipped over the shaft for winding while quills were stuck on the external end and wound outside. Quills and bobbins were kept in the box on top. This one dates from around 1850. $200-$300.

Generally known as a skein winder, the arms come out, allowing it to be stored easily. $65-$85.

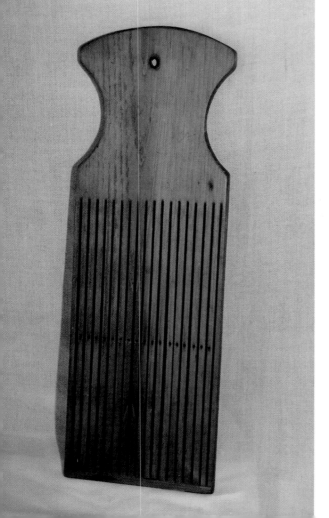

Tape looms are not too plentiful, nor are they that sought after. They do make attractive additions to fabric-making or needlecraft tool collections. $50-$75.

A favorite chair for the needlecrafter was the folding carpet rocker. One advantage of the rocker was the fact it could be folded for easy moving, like carrying it to a neighbors for a day of visiting and sewing. The carpet chair without rockers was a favorite for quilters. $100-$150.

Weavers from Peru made this poncho of llama wool using the branch frame or off-loom type weaving. $85-$150.

Close-up of the fabric and design.

Navajo-woven saddle blanket, now used as a rug. $300-$500.

Early sewing machine, the type used to sew some of the hand woven fabrics. $75-$100.

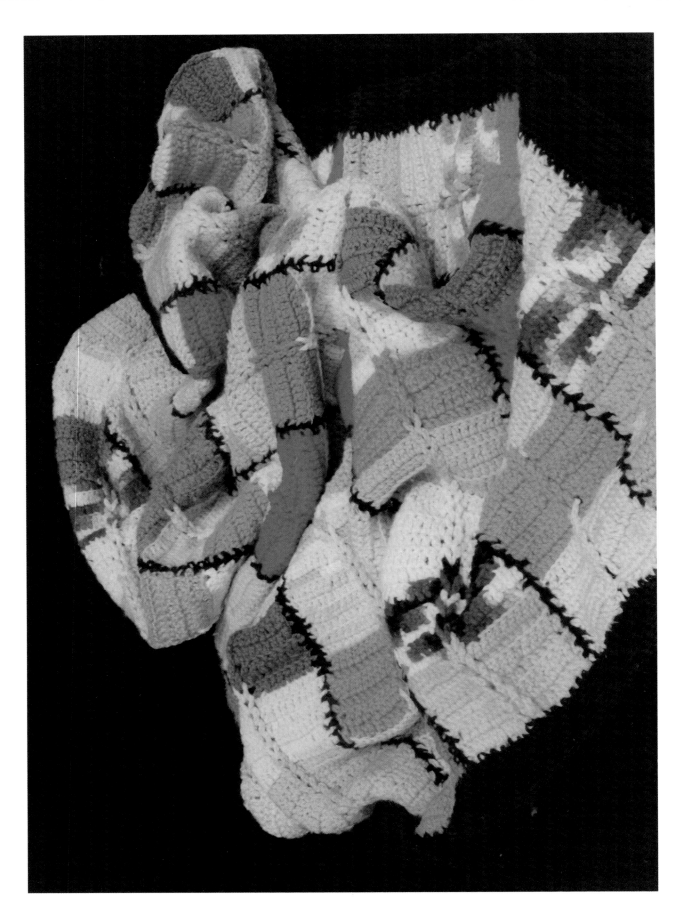

Needleworkers utilize every scrap of fabric or yarn. In this example, someone made an afghan. $25-$35. ·

Chapter 2
Afghans

The early vehicles, the wagons, buggies, and various types of carriages, did not have built-in heating systems. If they had any heat at all the family or the driver had to use some type of heater that could be a stone or a small foot stove. The small piece of soapstone with a bail type handle could be heated before the family left home, or they might prefer the small square foot stove made of wood and pierced tin that could be filled with hot coals. Heat from the latter would last longer and it could also be taken into their pew at church which was extremely helpful since some of the very early churches were not heated at all. Heavy carriage robes are believed to have been used long before the stones and the foot stoves as well as with them later. The history of the carriage robes probably goes back as far as the vehicle, especially in very cold climates. The carriage robe finally evolved into the so-called lap robe, a medium-sized wool or plush cover that was placed over the lap, hence the name. It was used to keep the passenger's feet and legs warm. The lap robe was also used in warmer climates and it continued to be used long after the newfangled automobiles replaced the horse and buggy, as the touring cars could be as cold or colder than the buggies even when curtains had been installed in the winter. Incidentally, the new sedans or closed cars weren't all that much warmer so the popularity of the lap robe continued

Both carriage robes and lap robes were being advertised well into this century. The choices and prices varied from wool lap robes priced from $2.50 to $25 while the imported plush robes were priced from $25 to $50 each. It is interesting now to find that in 1905 one could buy wool robes to match the lining of their carriages. The choice of colors was green, blue, brown, black, and wine.

Early on some of the more expensive cars probably had heaters, and by the mid 1930s the majority of all new cars came equipped with them. But some of the older ladies complained the cars weren't warm enough. So, when their lap robes wore out and they were unable to buy new ones due to the fact they were not as accessible as they had been previously, the older members of my family simply whipped out their trusty old crochet hooks and knitting needles to make a substitute for the lap robe that eventually became known as an afghan. A diligent search has failed to find any history on the afghan other than what we remember. Plenty of information can be found on how to make them and the various types that were being made in instruction booklets published in the 1940s and 1950s, but no history. At the risk of sounding like a broken record we have to repeat, "Our ancestors were an ingenious lot. If something was not available, they simply made a substitute." They were so accustomed to making things at home, lack of a lap robe didn't pose a serious problem.

And once they started making the afghans, ideas seemed to bubble up like a spring. By the mid-1950s all types of afghans were being made, everything from the embroidery-on-knitted ones to those made on various frames. One of the frames that became available during that time was the one called Weave It. Wool yarn was woven on this one to form approximately three inch squares that were later put together with yarn left attached to one end. Then someone discovered how easy it was to embroider a cross stitch design using a counted stitch method.

Somewhere in that long ago someone discovered how easy it was to use a hairpin and crochet some type of thread on it to form a long lacy strip. The strips could be left as they were, or they could be made into circles. As you might have guessed it soon became known as hairpin lace. But hairpins large enough to accommodate wool yarn were not available so a wooden devise that would serve the purpose was invented. Maybe the manufactured examples came first. It is known that several, including the homemade examples, have been seen. The Ez-Duz-It frame, which is very similar to the homemade example shown in the illustrations, was offered for sale for $1 in 1948. Another on the same style came out in 1954 and was called a Hairpin Lace Staple. Both were shaped very much like a hairpin, but much larger. All of them were used to make hairpin lace afghans.

Everybody has, at one time or another, had an idea for making an unusual afghan. An example is the one made to resemble the flag. The size may vary from the size of a twin bed sheet to a small throw size. The latter is still very popular with nursing home patients. Afghans are still being made today, and one great source for finding either an old or used one for sale is at a yard sale, church sale, or an estate auction where they are selling all the contents of the house. Depending on where you find it and how badly the person wants to sell, prices can vary from $5 to $50.

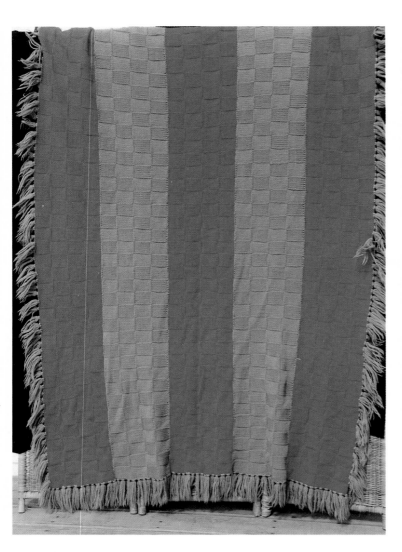

Gray and red knitted afghan. $30-$45.

A replica of the flag was knitted to make this afghan. $45-$65.

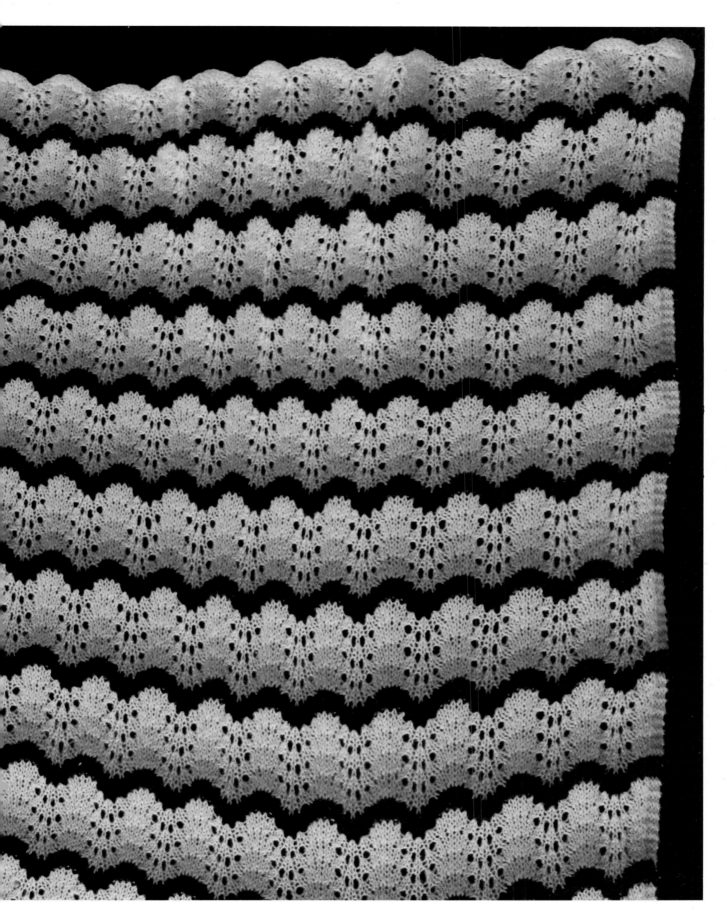

Light-weight afghan crocheted very loosely. $18-$27.

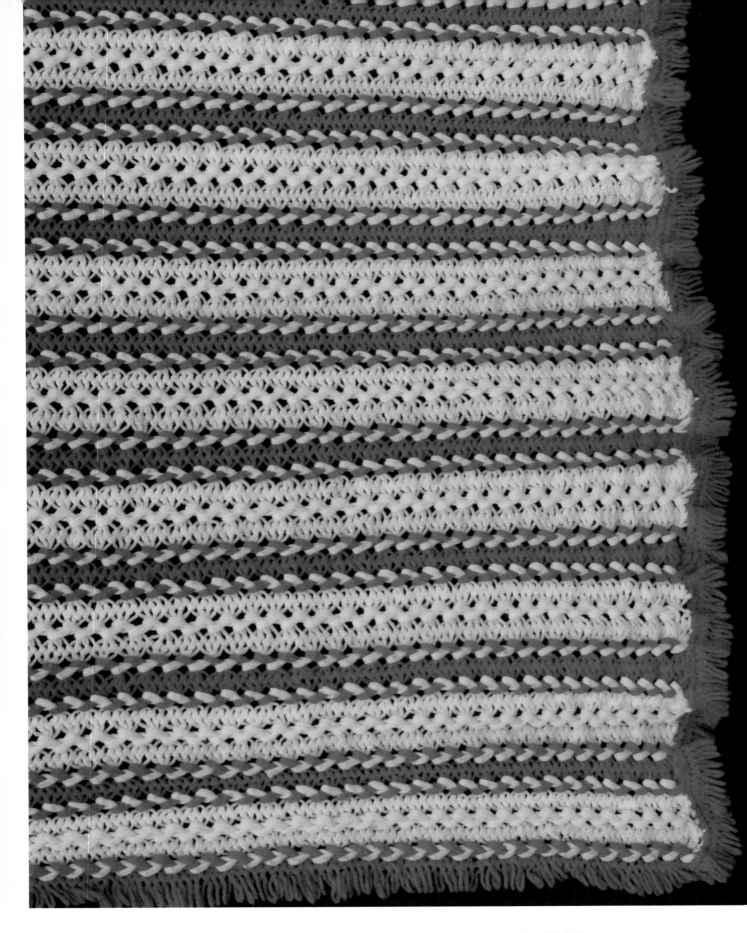

Afghan made on frame after the hairpin lace style. $35-$45.

Hairpins were not long enough nor strong enough to hold the wool yarn required to make afghans; therefore several companies made suitable frames. One was called Ez-Duz-It. In 1948 the frame was selling for $1, the instruction booklet for 25 cents.

Afghan made on Weave-It frame, then embroidered in counted cross-stitch. The design is larger due to the size of the yarn. $60-$95.

Small size afghan crocheted in white, pink, and blue. $18-$25

Another afghan made on Weave-It frame. This one has the
design woven in each square. $30-$50.

Knitted afghan with embroidery. Small size. $40-$60.

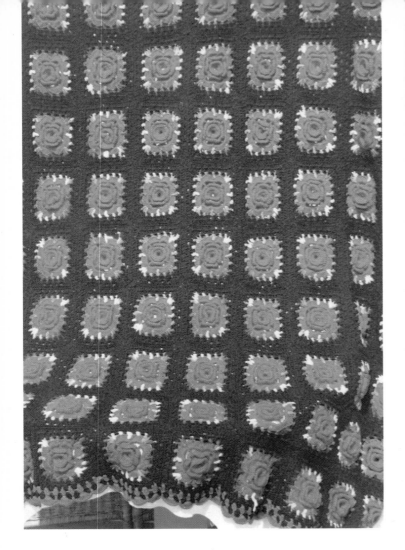

Crocheted rose afghans have been popular since the 1930s. $30-$45.

Close-up of crocheted rose design.

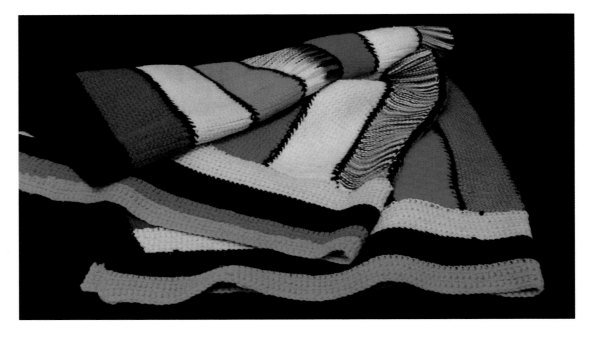

Attractive afghan with three-color border. $25-$40.

Maker used left-over yarn to crochet this one, then put the strips together very poorly. $18-$25.

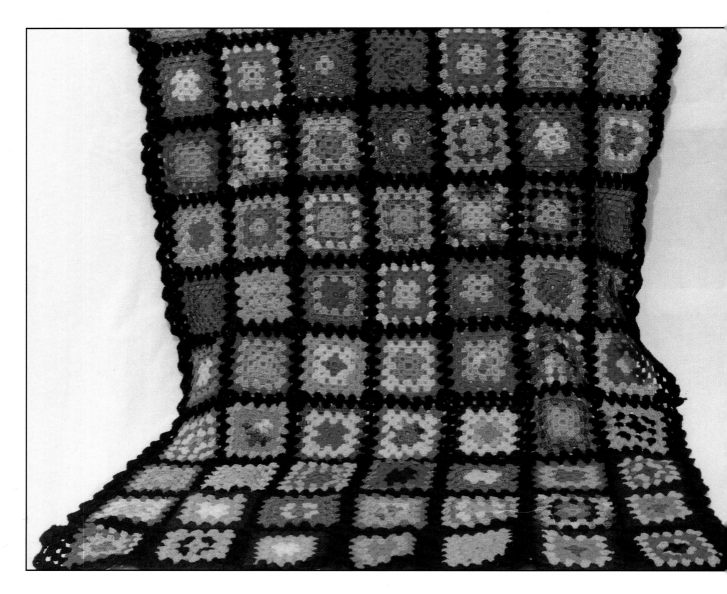

Afghan made with so-called Granny
Squares. $25-$30.

The colors used in this crocheted afghan
makes it most attractive. $35-$50.

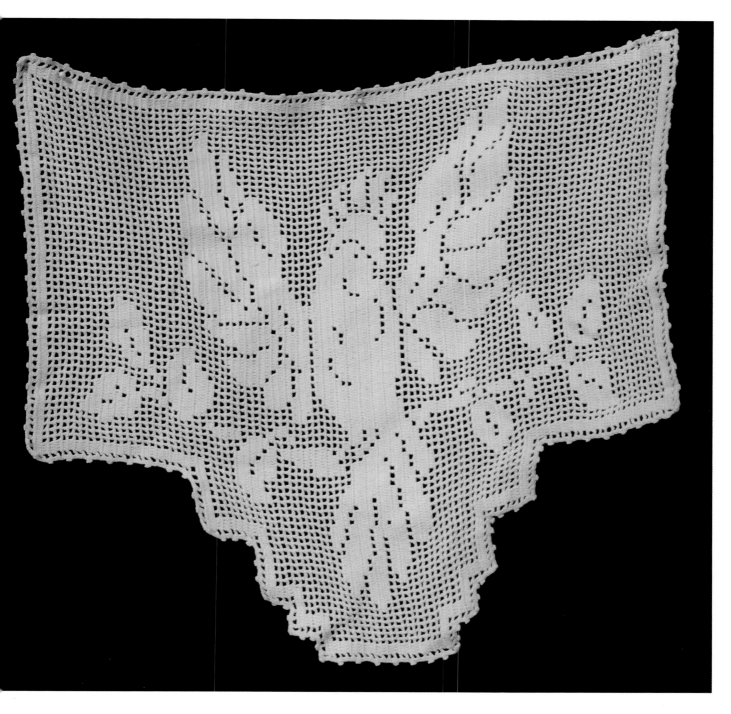

Birds were also a favorite design. This one is done in filet crochet. $9-$12.

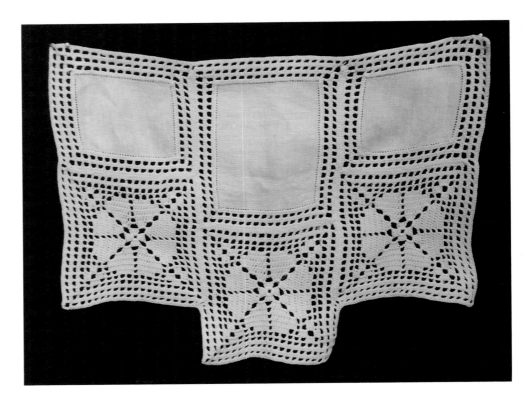

Plainer altar cloth with alternating crochet and linen. $8-$12.

Linen altar cloth with filet banner lined with red ribbon placed across diagonally. Heavily embroidered letter in same color as ribbon under crochet. $15-$20.

Altar cloth with cross and message No Cross No Crown.
Heavily fringed all around. $18-$25.

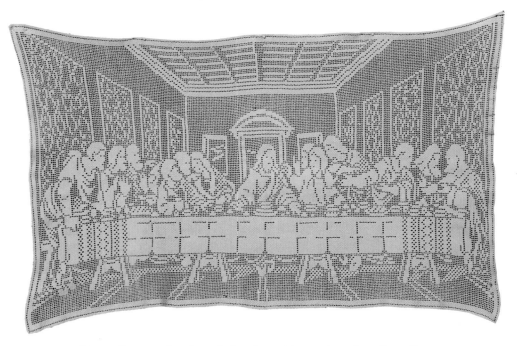

Depending on the size of the altar this crocheted replica of Leonardo da Vinci's painting of The Last Supper, sometimes called The Lord's Supper, could be used. $30-$50.

Due to the size, 40 by 50 inches, this crocheted replica of da Vinci's painting would have had to hang on the wall behind the altar. $35-$60.

Chapter 4
Bedspreads

It is only since quilts became so popular that bedspreads have received any recognition at all, yet they are as old, if not older, than quilts. Perhaps that is because handmade ones haven't been made for a half century or more, and then only on a very limited basis. Of course millions of factory-made bedspreads were made and shipped all over the country, but somehow factory made linens just don't seem to excite collectors like the handmade. Finding much information on them is quite difficult, but we did find that during the sixteenth century the word rug had two meanings in Britain. One referred to a "rough woollen material" that was suitable for winter mantles and cloaks while the other described it as "a large piece of thick woollen stuff used as a coverlet." Like those and so many later handmade bedspreads that were made to fit the needs of the maker, they were discarded when too worn for further use. Few, if any, records were ever kept because the style, type of stitches, and other pertinent information was passed from mother to daughter—by word of mouth.

It is believed the word bedspread just evolved from the term bed rug used by the Colonists. Regardless of the name, the bed rug and the bedspread have both had long and varied careers. The bed rug is known to have been in use in northern Europe during the fifteenth century, maybe earlier. And it was brought to America, if not by the Pilgrims, then by the ones who followed closely behind them. The best information on them can be found in old diaries, invoices, inventories, and wills. One example is the invoice that lists "240 yards ruggs for beds" that arrived in Massachusetts in 1636. Another record shows that "many Biscay rugs" were lost in 1626 when a French ship was destroyed on the coast

of what is now Maine. During that time, as the men were leaving England they were given a list of the essentials they would need in the Colonies. The Massachusetts Bay Company estimated the following would be necessary to furnish 100 men: "50 ruggs, 50 peare of blanketts of Welsh cotton, 100 peare of sheets, 50 bedtykes & bolsters."

As proof America was growing rapidly there are records that around 1630 ships were bringing in as many as "9 Irish rugs for beds" each trip. It seems that those who could afford it bought English rugs for themselves and Irish rugs for the servants. We have to understand the use of some words to be able to understand the records as one tells of twenty families of experienced clothmakers settling in Massachusetts around 1640. They were, it says, "making cloath and ruggs of cotton wool, and also sheep's wooll." Apparently the wool from the sheep was considered a better wool as it required two ls in the spelling. Since it was so early after the Pilgrims arrived, they had not had time to raise enough sheep to furnish the clothmakers with wool so it was shipped in from Spain while the cotton wool came from the West Indies.

We tend to think that all early bedrugs were heavily embroidered in bright colored yarns as the few we have seen in museums are of this type, but there were white ones, probably similar to the factory-made ones used so extensively during the nineteenth century. This theory is based on a few wills that have listed "white ruggs."

Then in the 1800s many of the wills and inventories found in Knox County, Tennessee, listed bedspreads as bedspreads. The first example was the sale of the estate of a Dr. Parker. Among the items sold was a bedspread that brought $1.70. A feather bed sold for $14.00. During the October term of court in 1869 still in Knox County the estate of a Mr. Hickum was sold. The listings include three beds, all with "covers." There is no description of the covers but it is assumed they were the usual for each bed, a pair of sheets, either a blanket or a quilt, and a bedspread. It is questionable whether or not pillow cases and/or bolsters were included as in most of the wills and inventories they were listed separately and sold for good prices. No description was given of the beds and all sold with covers. The prices realized in the Hickum sale was $7.00, 9.00, and $10.00 per bed. At that same sale two quilts sold for 25 cents (for both) while a blanket and sheet brought $3.60.

Almost from the beginning girls in this country worked steadily and regularly on household linens for their dower chest. By the time they were married they might have several chests filled with the finest of handmade linens. This custom continued into the first decades of this century. The girls took pride in making elegant things for their new home, and the workmanship on all the pieces, especially the bedspreads, was exquisite. They made both summer and winter bedspreads and covered them with embroidery, some all white, others in a variety of colors. They made some that were bands of vertical crochet alternating with bands of linen of the same size and shape, and then there were the solidly crocheted or knitted bedspreads. Shortly before the turn of this century a variety of needlework magazines hit the market. This was new for the women as many had not had too much information or new ideas for their needlework previously. The magazines not only offered new ideas, but printed patterns and designs along with directions that could be used on all types of household linens. At that time there were no radios, television, or movies. The only entertainment was an occasional quilting bee, a barn raising, and church suppers. This meant their long, winter evenings could be devoted to their needlework, and in New England those evenings could be especially long in winter. That is one of the reasons so many household linens can still be found there.

However, New England was not the only place where the women did excessive amounts of needlework. It was being done all over the country, but apparently on a lesser scale. After all, the women in the south had shorter, warmer nights which meant the weather permitted them to enjoy more social activities. Nevertheless those southern ladies filled their dower chest as full as their northern cousins. Incidentally, the name of the dower chest even-

tually changed to hope chest, a term that continued to be used well into the 1950s in some areas.

Nobody seems to know where the Knotted Bedspread method originated. Some seem to believe it began in England and Scotland, but no proof of that can be found. Those who believe it originated in those countries believe it was brought into America by the first settlers. Again there is little or no proof, but it can't be denied the spreads were being made in Pennsylvania and New England over a century and a half to two centuries ago. This writer remembers well watching skilled needleworkers making the knotted bedspreads in the Great Smokey Mountains area 35 to 40 years ago. They told of relatives in the Blue Ridge Mountains who were making the same type bedspreads. When asked how they learned to make the knotted spreads they immediately told of some relative, usually a grandmother who "had always made them." This was another case of directions being passed from mother to daughter for generations without any thought of ever putting it in writing.

Until after the turn of the present century those mountains were one of the most isolated areas in the country. Many of the settlers had moved there from Pennsylvania and New England shortly after their arrival in this country. They kept the old ways and the old customs, so it is very possible this method of bedspread-making originated in England and Scotland where many of the settlers originated.

Perhaps the most appealing thing about the spreads was the fact they could be made from materials which were readily available on the farm, such as flour sacks that had been washed and bleached in the sun. With the large families most people had at that time it was not unusual for them to buy a hundred pounds of flour at a time. This meant the bag or sack was made of strong white fabric. Later they might use the white feed or grain sacks, or by that time they might have money to buy unbleached muslin. One worker told about her great grandmother weaving fabric, linsey-woolsey fabric, on the family loom to make the Knotted spreads. Others told of taking old linsey-woolsey sheets they no longer used and decorating them with knotting to make bedspreads. Unlike the quilts and coverlets these bedspreads were made more for decorative use than for warmth. The decoration or the knotting was done with cotton yarn. Some of the less affluent used the strings or thread used to sew up all types of bags like flour sacks, feed sacks, or anything else that came in fabric bags that had been sewn with cotton thread. The French knots were used to create designs on the bedspreads. Some

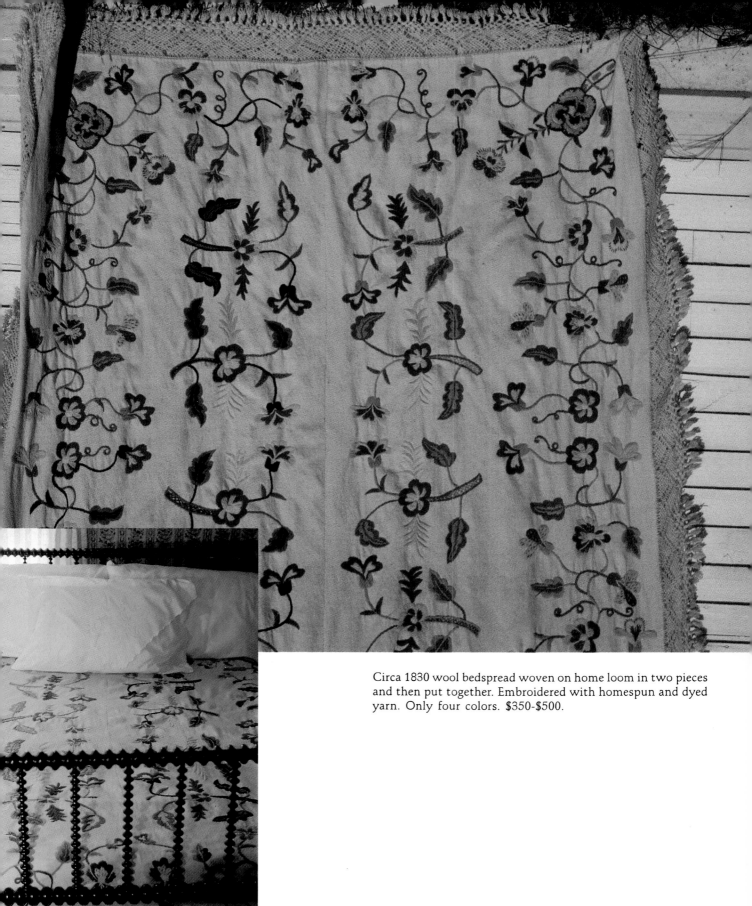

Circa 1830 wool bedspread woven on home loom in two pieces and then put together. Embroidered with homespun and dyed yarn. Only four colors. $350-$500.

Same bedspread on bed.

Close-up showing the lace border made of the same undyed yarn.

Knitted bedspread with matching lace border. $150-$225.

Crocheted bedspread, heavy yarn. $125-$150.

Corner of crocheted bedspread with house in center. Crocheted ruffle around the edge. Small size would indicate it was made for a young girl's bed. $175-$200.

Thin summer bedspread, embroidered. $95-$110.

Close-up of filet crochet house in center of bedspread.

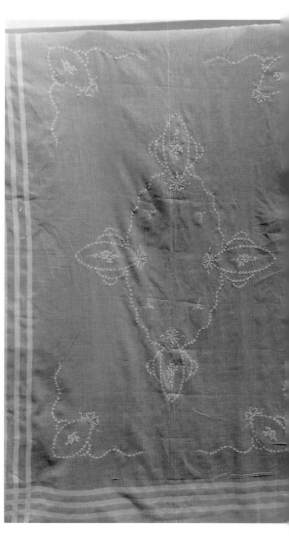

Alternating strips of crochet and heavy linen were used to make this bedspread. $85-$115.

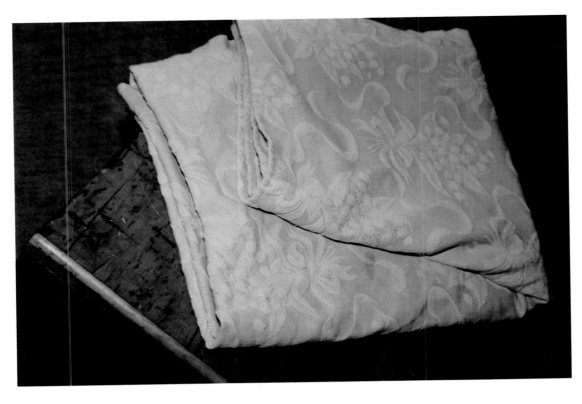

Bates Manufacturing Company, Lewiston, Maine, introduced their all-cotton jacquard weave bedspreads around 1915. $20-$45.

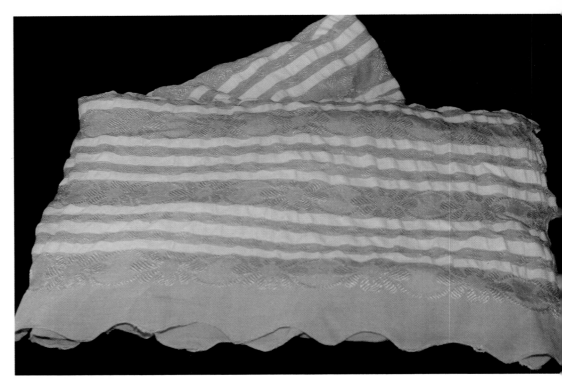

This cotton rayon blend made an excellent summer bedspread. When Bates introduced this one they called it Ripplette. $20-$35.

In 1871 when Bates Manufacturing Company, Lewiston Maine, introduced their new line of "Marseilles quilts" they stressed the fact they used the names quilt and bedspread interchangeably. Unless the label is still on the bedspread, it may not necessarily be a Bates. To make it even more confusing, Bates was advertising the fact they were making 800 different styles of fabrics and bedspreads that year. $80-$110.

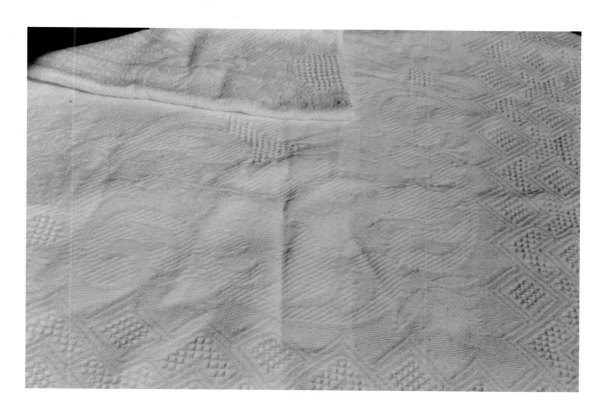

Another Marseilles bedspread. $75-$90.

Marseilles bedspread for poster bed. $85-$110.

Knotted bedspread with all-over design. $95-$150.

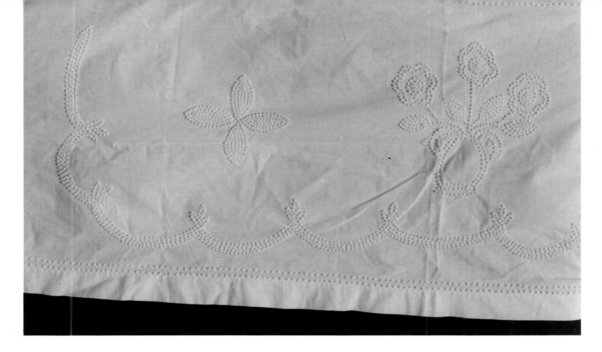

Separate knotted bolster to use with matching bedspread. Unfortunately, most bedspreads and bolsters were separated through the years, making it difficult to match them now. Bolster only $40-$75.

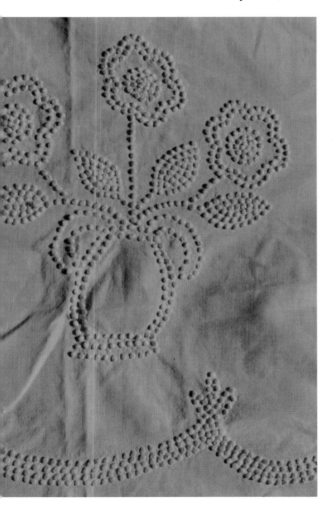

End of bolster showing the netting-type lace that was so popular for knotted bedspreads.

se-up of one of the designs in the bolster.

Opposite page:
Another knotted bedspread design. $100-$200.

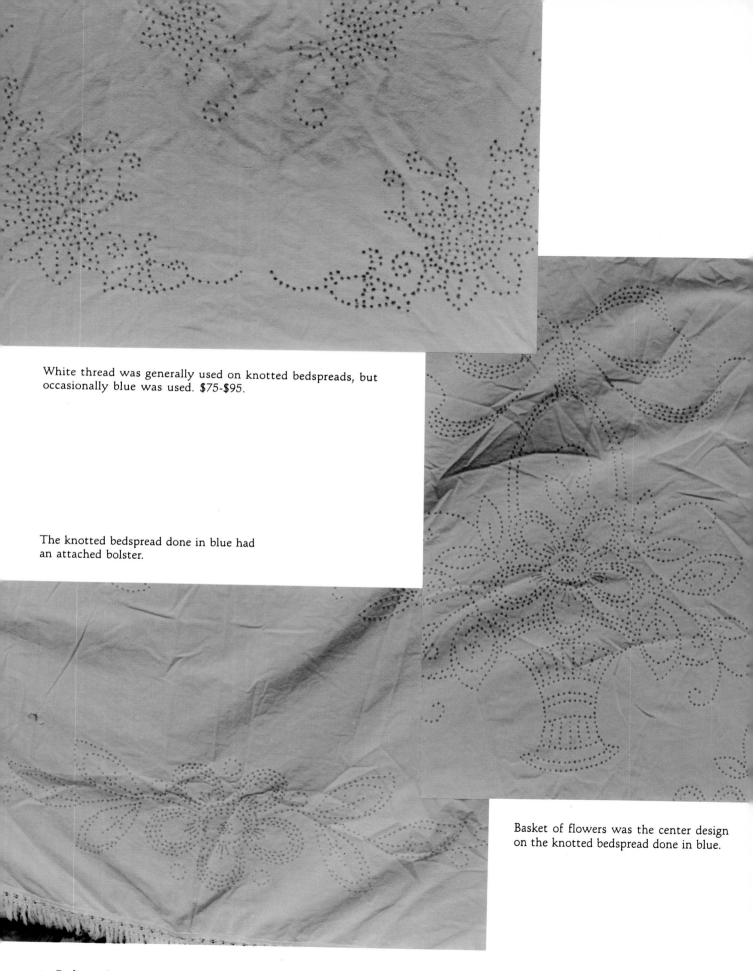

White thread was generally used on knotted bedspreads, but occasionally blue was used. $75-$95.

The knotted bedspread done in blue had an attached bolster.

Basket of flowers was the center design on the knotted bedspread done in blue.

One hundred pound flour sacks like this one were often used to make knotted bedspreads. $5-$10.

Light weight Marseilles bedspread with matching bolster. $95-$150.

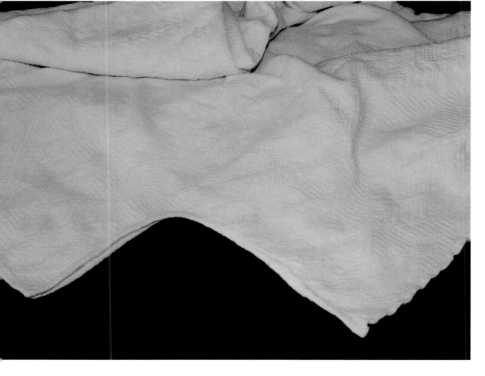

Plain, light weight Marseilles bedspread for poster bed. $75-$115.

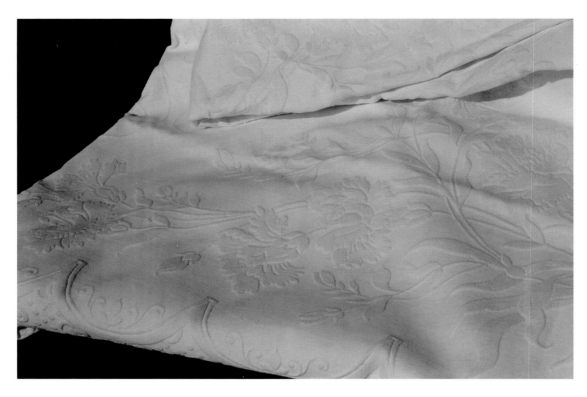

Bedspread with beautiful design. $100-$150.

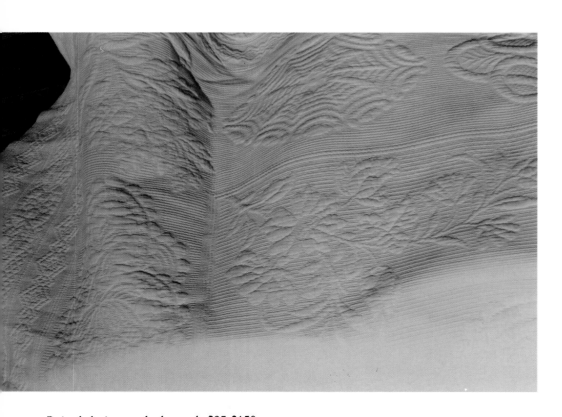

Raised design on bedspread. $95-$150.

White factory woven bedspread. $95-$150.

Red and white chenille bedspread. $25-$40.

Chenille bedspread in several shades of blue. $25-$35.

Center of blue chenille bedspread.

Late Battenberg bedspread handmade in China. $75-$95.

Chapter 5
Centerpieces

The words centerpiece and doily are almost interchangeable today simply because most of us either don't know or can't remember exactly how they were made and used originally. For nearly a century, from about 1850 to 1940, Americans had an entirely different lifestyle than what we enjoy now. In the beginning there were no distractions such as automobiles, movies, or television, and until the late 1940s few women had jobs outside the home, and many of them had a maid or maids. This left them with ample time to concentrate on their homes. Perhaps to stay busy and certainly to be able to compete with their peers, they made an abundance of household linens. This in turn meant they had to do lots of home entertaining to be able to show off their handiwork. So, began the days of gracious living and grand entertaining.

Many of the women made household linens according to tradition, that is, they used the same styles and designs as their mothers and grandmothers. In time various magazines, especially the needlecraft ones began publication and they were filled with information and directions the women could use. Then there were women like my grandmother who simply could not read and understand directions for crochet, yet she could look at any completed piece and copy it exactly. Nor was she too concerned with what fashion decreed. If she bought a new table or chest, she simply got out her sewing basket and crocheted a centerpiece to fit— one that she decided was right for that piece of furniture. Later she would make others in different designs, maybe one with an embroidered center and crocheted lace around the outside. She was also one of the first people I ever knew who used a large round centerpiece over the white damask tablecloth on the dining room table. The table was long to accommodate all the children and grandchildren who usually visited each weekend. She said the long table covered entirely in white was monotonous so to break that monotony she kept a large, round centerpiece embroidered in bright colors in the center of the table topped with a vase of flowers from her garden.

Technically that piece could have passed for a doily as well as a centerpiece because it seems the doily was supposed to be used under something while the centerpiece covered something. Today collectors don't seem to be too concerned with whether the piece was made originally for one use or the other, and truthfully it is sometimes next to impossible to determine the use of each unless the pieces have been passed down through the family or someone still remembers how they were used. When two or more small pieces exactly alike are found, it is usually an indication they originated as doilies. But that is not always the case. The centerpiece just seems to have evolved; it was needed to cover tables and therefore it was made. It may be round, square, oblong or diamond shaped, and it will still be a centerpiece. It may be crocheted, tatted, knitted, or embroidered, and it is still a centerpiece. It can be used any way the owner desires, or needs. Centerpieces were such an important part of the household linens, the housewife usually had one or more envelope type holders in which to store them. It too was usually covered in embroidery.

Opposite page:
Crocheted centerpieces are especially attractive when used with fall foliage.

It is difficult now for collectors to settle on a particular type of centerpiece because there is such a variety available. They were made in such a assortment of sizes, colors, fabrics, and types of needlework. Some were made specifically for use on the so-called center table, especially the oak ones that came with the oak living rooms suites, those that were so popular from around the turn of the present century to as late as the 1950s in some areas. Prior to that time there had been the gorgeous little tables and the bedside commodes, but indications are centerpieces weren't as necessary on them as the later oak tables. The majority of the centerpieces were made to fit the needs as well as the whims of the homemaker. She made the final decision on what and how all the needlework would be used.

It's true that during that period needlework became one of the most popular gifts for exchange. Everybody had plenty and they loved dividing with friends and family. But if the piece didn't fit the recipient's needs or decor, it was quietly packed away until it could be passed on to someone else. There was a lot of gift giving in those days. Then as now a lot depended on desirability and that hinged on the skills of the maker. Some of the pieces were exquisitely done while some should never have been made. An example of this is shown in the illustrations. Two round cloths have been found that are identical in size and design. One was embroidered with silk thread which was perfect for this cloth while the other was done with two strands of cotton thread rather than three or maybe four on a design this large. Apparently the maker wasn't skilled enough to know she needed larger thread, but realized something was wrong and abandoned the project before it was completed. When looking at the completed centerpiece it becomes quite obvious how much tatted lace adds to any piece.

Even though it is sometimes difficult to distinguish between the centerpieces and doilies, it is possible that today's collectors are more concerned with the condition and workmanship than the original use. Like our ancestors who made what appealed to them and what they needed, collectors should do the same. They should collect the pieces that appeal to them and pieces that fit their needs.

Hardanger embroidery required special fabric, skill, and patience, but it produced some of the most beautiful needlework. Scarce now and rather expensive. $45-$75.

Corner of centerpiece showing work in
greater detail.

Close-up of Hardanger centerpiece with
different design. $35-$50.

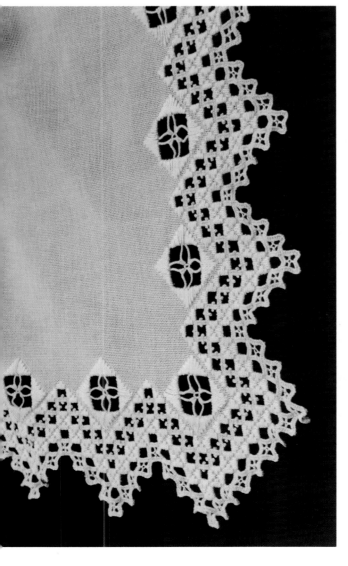

Corner of white Hardanger centerpiece
with less ornate design. $30-$45.

Creamy beige Hardanger centerpiece with row of embroidery above the edge. $35-$55.

Close-up of the work.

Square Hardanger centerpiece with different design. $35-$55.

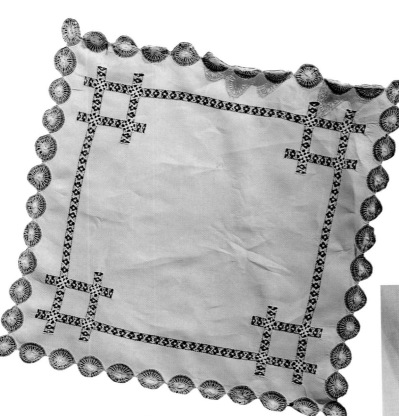

Two different types of needlework was used on this centerpiece. It has drawn work in the center and hairpin lace edging. $20-30.

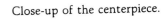

Close-up of the centerpiece.

To make drawn work the worker had to pull the threads from the fabric one way, and with those threads work a design on the remaining threads. $20-$35.

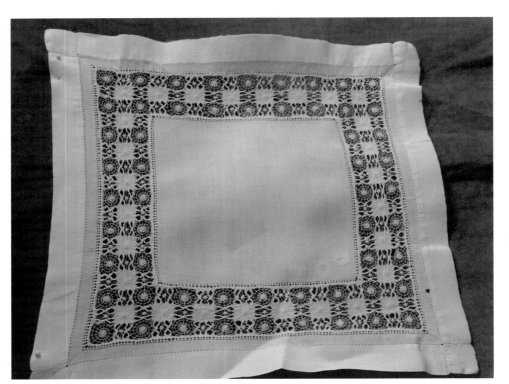

Square drawn work centerpiece. $17-$2[...]

Centerpiece with plainer drawn work design. $12-$20.

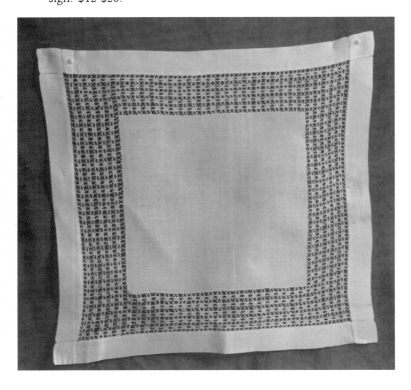

Oblong centerpiece with both drawn work and embroidery. Could also double as tea cart cover. $23-$35.

White-on-white embroidered linen centerpiece. $16-$20.

Cord or braid embroidered centerpiece. The braid was used to make the design. $10-$15.

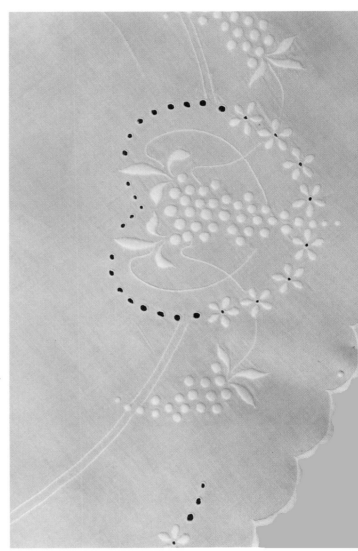

Close-up of grape design used on white-on-white piece.

Small linen centerpiece with heavy embroidery. $12-$19.

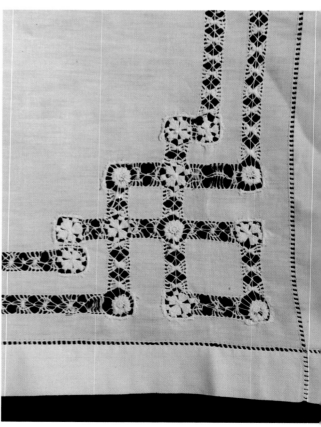

Close-up of one corner of the piece.

Small linen centerpiece with fancy drawn work design. $18-$25.

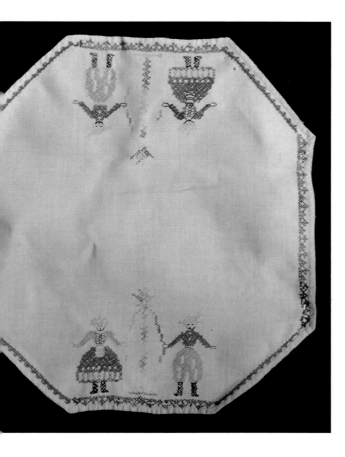

Dutch boy and girl embroidered using two strands of thread, which makes a weak design. $9-$12.

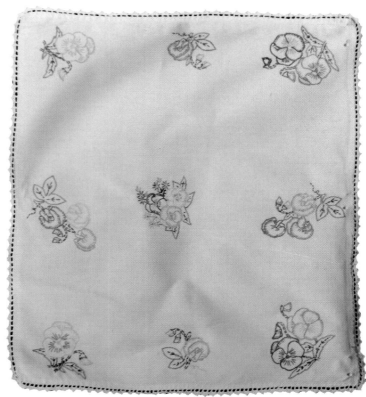

Centerpiece with pansy and sweet pea design done in colors. Circa 1950. $9-$14.

Close-up of pansy and sweet pea design.

Another late centerpiece done in colors. $7-$10.

This piece could easily be used as a centerpiece or a tea cart cover. $12-$15.

White-on-white embroidered centerpiece.
$12-$15.

Centerpiece with embroidered butterfly
design. $14-$19.

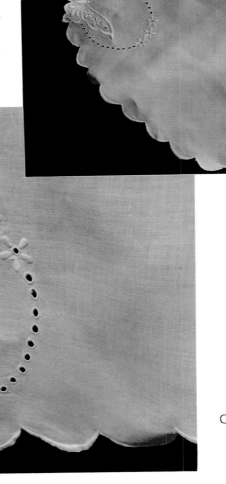

Close-up of butterfly design.

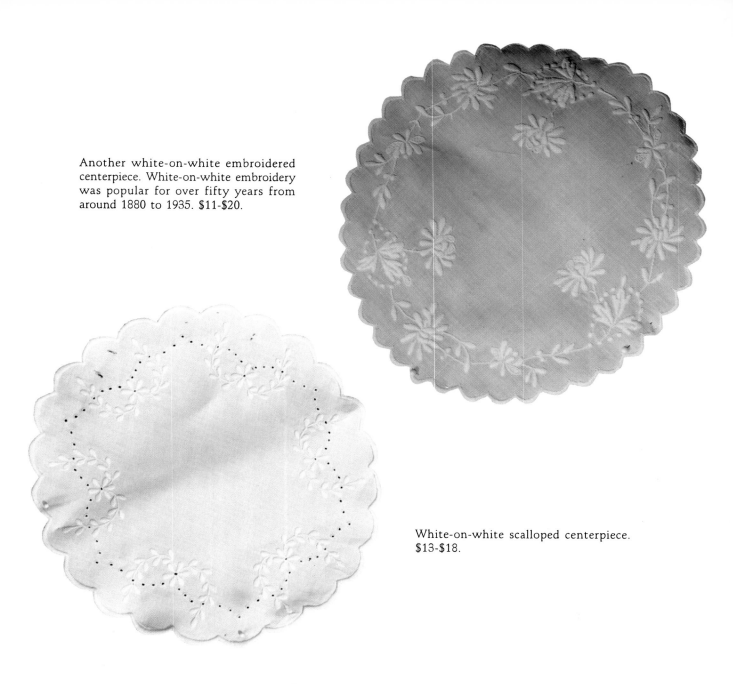

Another white-on-white embroidered centerpiece. White-on-white embroidery was popular for over fifty years from around 1880 to 1935. $11-$20.

White-on-white scalloped centerpiece. $13-$18.

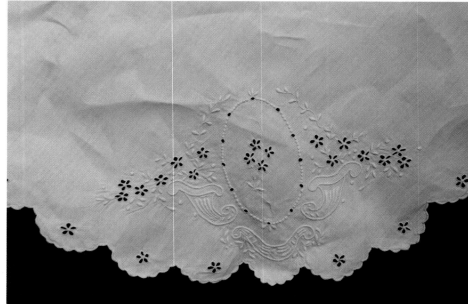

One of three designs that appear around this centerpiece. $12-$15.

Hardanger centerpiece done in pink. $35-$50.

Round beige/gray centerpiece embroidered in green and white. $16-$22.

White centerpiece embroidered with blue thread. $10-$14.

Pair of crocheted curtains. $30-$45.

Chapter 6
Curtains and Shade Pulls

The very first houses built in America, those in Virginia and Massachusetts, had such tiny windows they didn't require curtains. As the houses grew larger so did the windows, and the need for some kind of window covering became very apparent. Then as the southern planters and merchants began building their so-called mansions, some with floor to ceiling windows, the need and the demand for coverings for those windows grew larger. The purpose of the drapes and curtains was three-fold. First, it kept people on the outside from seeing the people on the inside, especially when those people inside might be taking a bath or dressing. It was found later that shades could serve the same purpose without opening and closing the drapes on a daily basis. It also kept the bright sunlight from fading the upholstery and fine rugs. And last but not least it made the plain windows so much more attractive, both inside and out.

Chances of the average collector finding any of those fine old drapes, in good condition, is very remote. However it is very helpful to know something about the fabrics used then. In their 1891 catalog Jordan Marsh and Company, Boston, Massachusetts, listed "a larger line of art fabrics for special orders." They didn't specify it, but it was obvious these fabrics could be special ordered for special customers, fabrics like Brocatelles, Satin Derbys, Silk and Mohair Plushes, English and French Tapestries, single and double faced Velours, Satin Damask, and many rare French Novelties in the latest designs and colorings. These are all luxury fabrics and one can only imagine how beautifully they would make up into drapes. The same fabric could be used to upholster the furniture which would make the room even more beautiful. Other curtain fabrics offered that year were China silks that were suggested "expressly for Mantel Draperies, Bed Canopies, Screen Panels, Bookcases (probably curtain-like panels for the inside of the bookcase doors), and Sash Curtains."

Lace curtains have always been extremely popular, so it was not a surprise to find dozens of different types advertised in the Jordan Marsh catalog. One of the extra features of the lace curtains that year, they said, was the increased use of sash curtains described as popular "little French curtains." They were carrying a full line in stock that year with many to match the full length lace curtains including Antique, Cluny, Irish Point, and Brussels. A few pairs of these old lace curtains have been seen, some with matching bedspreads, and there is absolutely no comparison between them and the later so-called lace curtains used so frequently during the first half of this century. Price alone should point out the difference. The later curtains, those used by the average family from around 1925 to about 1950, cost around 75 cents to $3 a pair while the Cluny curtains started at $2 and went to $40 a pair. And that was 1891. Brussels lace curtains were priced from $12 to $75 a pair in the Jordan Marsh catalog. By 1908 Sears, Roebuck & Company was advertising Brussels Net curtains for a cheaper price and they could have been a cheaper quality as well because Jordan Marsh described their curtains as lace whereas Sears used the term net. However the Sears curtains were priced $3.95 a pair and described as "prettiest and daintiest shown this season." They also said they would make handsome parlor curtains, only came in white, and were 3 yards long and 48 inches wide.

For some reason probably only known to the architect, the doors in those old houses were extremely wide. They might have sliding or pocket doors, but when they were closed, the rooms could be very dark as most had dark furniture and even darker paneling. For that reason the French portieres became very popular. They not only reduced the width of the doors, but when they were made of the same fabric as the drapes they were very attractive. In 1891 Jordan Marsh offered all chenille portieres with extra heavy fringe at both ends for $5.50 a pair. Figured double-faced velours were priced $40 a pair while silk Sheila ones were as high as $50 a pair.

By 1913 text books were being used in the schools to teach the girls the latest in shelter and clothing. One of the first things being taught was that "heavy dust-catching draperies, long curtains, and hangings" formerly used in so many homes was slowly giving way to simpler forms, that is shorter curtains and drapes as well as lighter fabrics. They were suggesting fabrics like poplins, casement cloth, soft silks, denims, and arras. Solid colors as well as figured materials like old-fashioned English chintzes, cretonnes, and block printed linens were recommended. They also said that the long clumsy lace curtains weren't as popular as they had been; they were being replaced by inexpensive fabrics like madras, serim, cheesecloth, lawn, swiss, and linen. Stenciling rugs and walls was already popular and they suggested the homemaker might stencil curtains made of pongee, scrim, and muslin.

It was about that time that the women decided to make some of their curtains. Two factors probably prompted this decision. First and foremost was the fact they could make something unusual, something that was different from that made by their friends. The second reason could have been money. Buying their own fabric, especially if they were going to embroider their curtains, was cheaper than ready-made curtains. And if she were going to crochet them, balls of thread were also cheaper. Still in the handmade curtain category there are discoveries that actually keep you awake at night wondering when, why, and for what purpose certain pairs of curtains were made. An example of this is shown in one of the illustrations which shows a pair of linen curtains, one of only three found, that are made entirely by hand, every single, tiny stitch including the band for the rod that was sewn on the back of the pleats. The top is 11 inches wide and they are 61 inches long. The only logical solution seems to be the maker had a sun porch with long narrow windows. When she no longer needed

Attractive pair, 1930s, factory-made lace curtains. When found, these will usually have some damage. $9-$12 pair.

them she could have given some pairs to a friend o family member, or the sun could have rotted the fabric in the other pairs. Apparently she was very proud of her handiwork as she embroidered (satin stitched) her initials on one side of one of the curtains.

Window shades could be bought or they could be homemade. Unless the homemaker was very tal ented or simply preferred to make her own shades they were usually bought ready made. The olde window shades are difficult to find and very few people want them when they are found. But around the turn of the present century, and as late as the fifties, homemakers delighted in making crocheted or tatted shade pulls. The pulls were fastened abou the middle of the shade and looked very attractive hanging between the curtains. The pulls were s small and of such little importance to people who were skilled with their needles, they didn't give thought to discarding them. After all, if they eve needed more they could make them easily and quickly. A few years ago these pulls could be foun rather easily, but in the last few years they have become quite scarce.

Pair of handmade linen curtains embroidered in red. $30-$40.

Pair of circa 1940, factory-made lace curtains. Fabric is very weak, hence the price. $9-$12 pair.

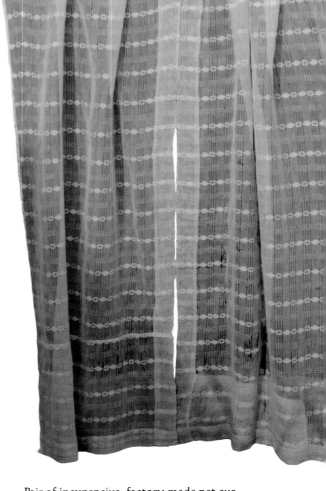

Pair of inexpensive, factory-made net curtains from around 1940. $10-$14 a pair in good condition.

Bottom design on factory-made curtains.

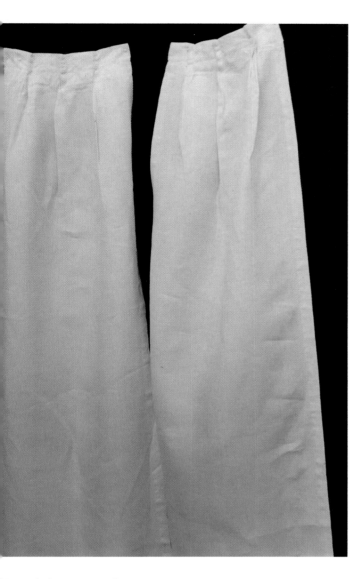

Only one panel of these curtains was found. It was found in a mall with a price tag that described it as a dresser scarf. Someone probably bought the other panel to use that way. $20-$30 pair.

One of three pairs of handmade, heavy linen drapes. Made with very tiny stitches, each done by hand. $25-$35 pair.

Apparently the maker was proud of her curtains as she embroidered her initials on them.

Bottom of curtain panel showing the cross-stitch embroidery in greater detail.

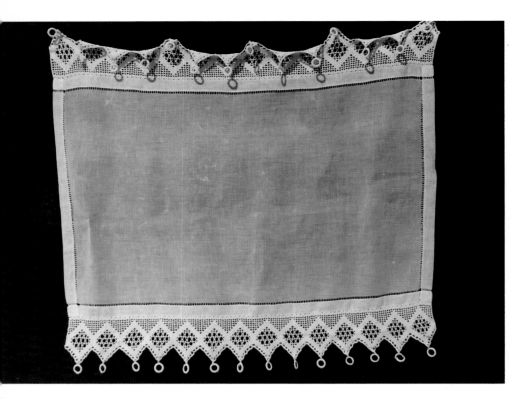

The majority of Victorian homes had heavy front doors, half wood, half glass. The glass portion had to be covered with a curtain or curtains. This is an example of such curtains. It is handmade with crocheted top and bottom, including the rings for the rod. $15-$20.

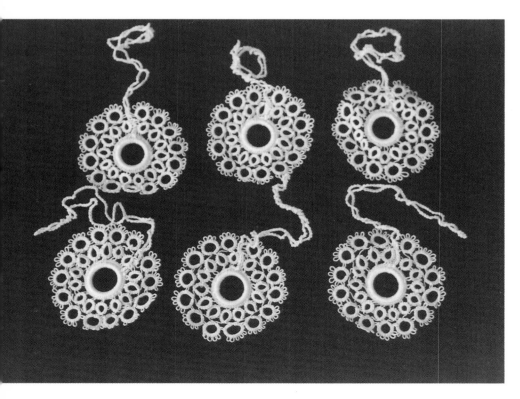

Since each room or maybe all rooms in the house had the same type of shade pulls, it is not unusual now to find them in lots of six or twelve. Tassel shade pulls like this one make excellent key holders. The long cord makes them easy to find and to hang on key boards. Six for $10.

Six, hard-to-find, tatted shade pulls. Six for $15-$23.

Pair of crocheted shade pulls. Six for $10-$13.

Pull on the left is the same design as the pair above, but the workmanship is much better. Six in either design $14-$18.

Four plain, crocheted shade pulls. Poor workmanship attaching the cords. Six for $6-$8.

Shade pulls crocheted in yet another design. Six for $9-$11.

Crocheted shade pulls in another design. Six for $9-$11.

A worker skilled in crochet could vary the designs to create new ones. Either style, six for $10-$12.

Embroidered deer and trees decorate this wool-on-wool pillow. $45-$55.

Decorative pillows have always been a must for wicker porch swings.

Needlepoint has always been a favorite for pillow makers. $25-$40.

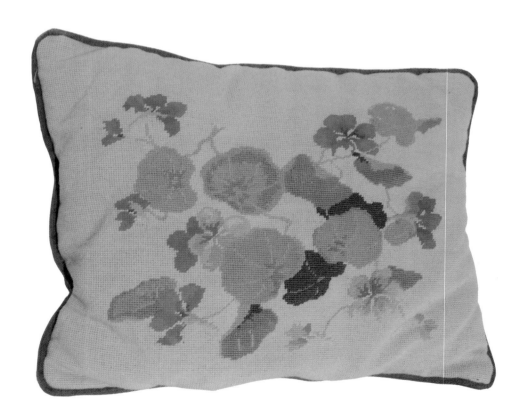

Nasturtium form the design for this needlepoint pillow. $25-$40.

Needlepoint pillow done with outdoor design—deer head with antlers. $18-$25.

Open cotton bolls form the design for this pillow done in needlepoint. $33-$40.

Needlepoint pillows were and still are very attractive on antique sofas and loveseats.

Fancy woven wool fabric with embroidery. $14-$17.

Same woolen fabric but different embroidered design. $15-$20.

Embroidered pillow. $10-$14.

Pillow with rows of birds and flowers cross-stitched down either side. $11-$15.

Birds were embroidered on this pillow. $10-$14.

Colors and workmanship are good on this
heavily embroidered pillow. $18-$25.

Pillow with cross stitched design. $12-
$17.

Green velvet pillow with white linen circle embroidered and
edged with crocheted lace. $17-$24.

Old quilt square made into a pillow. Blue and white ticking that holds the feathers can be seen through the white. $23-$30.

A square from a decade old quilt was used to make this pillow. It can be used on the bed with the quilt. $18-$25.

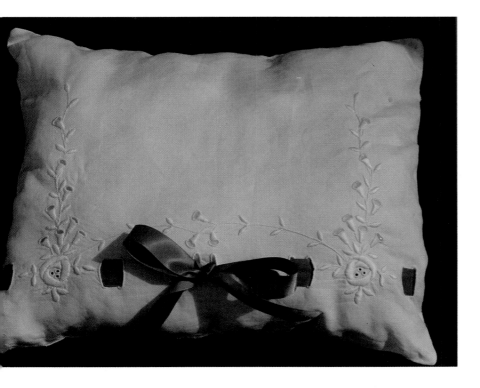

Embroidered white-on-white pillow laced with lavender ribbon. Definitely a bedroom pillow. $18-$23.

Yo-Yo pillow was probably made to be used with a matching Yo-Yo quilt. $20-$25.

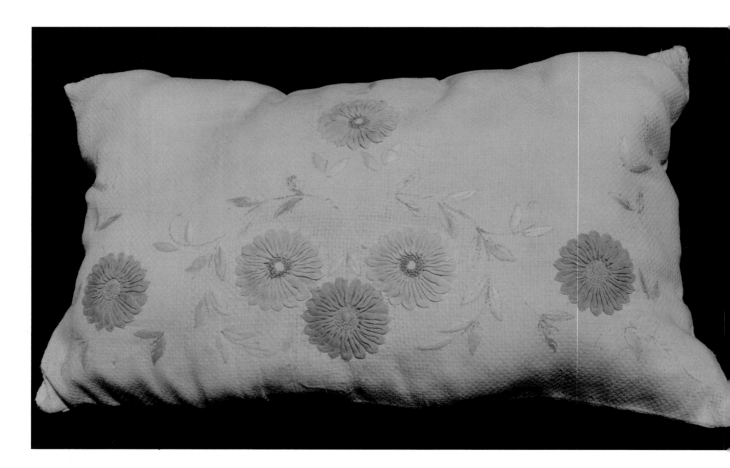

All types of needlework was used to make pillows. Rococo or China ribbon embroidery was used to make this one. $25-$35.

Using the old crazy quilt idea someone made this pillow. The silk ruffle around the pillow naturally identifies it as one for the parlor. $24-$30.

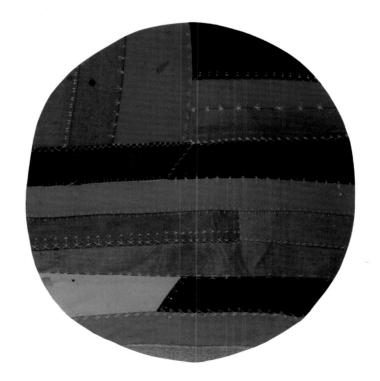

A similar idea was used to make this plain pillow. Is very attractive in an old captain-type chair. $10-$12.

Strange design for crocheted pillow top. $15-$28.

Pillow with simple crocheted top. $16-$20.

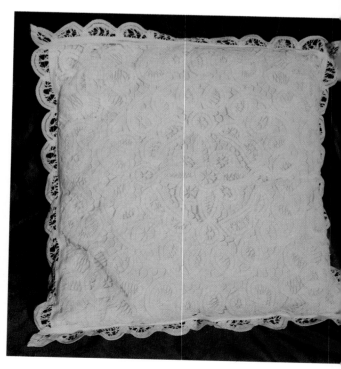

Late Battenberg lace pillow was made in China. $12-$17.

Pink lining makes this cut work pillow much more attractive. $23-$27.

What is a porch without wicker furniture (in the South), or wicker furniture without pillows.

Fancy green and pink crocheted doily, more decorative than useful. $10-$15.

Chapter 8
Doilies

Several factors have been combined to really confuse collectors about doilies and centerpieces. One was the luncheon set that combined the two. They might be crocheted, knitted, tatted, embroidered, or a combination of stitches. In the June 1924 issue of *The Modern Priscilla* there was a brief introduction and directions for crocheting a six piece luncheon set. They began by saying that the pieces "must be done of such a texture they will lie flat on the table and retain their shape through repeated launderings." The leaf motif was omitted from the "oval doilies" which meant they weren't identical in the beginning and are even harder to match now. They did offer this information: "When hot plates are used, asbestos mats [some other material would be best today] should be placed under the doilies to protect the table top." And then the confusion really begins because the first directions were for making an 18-inch centerpiece presumably for the center of the table. The next was for a 12-inch doily—or centerpiece indicating that size could have some bearing on whether it was a centerpiece or a doily. The next was a 8.5 inch plate doily while a 7-inch one was to be used for the bread and butter plate. Tumblers required 5-inch doily and there were directions for an 8 by 15 inch oval, no use given.

Another factor having a tremendous bearing on today's confusion would be the number of doilies—and centerpieces that were made over the years. We only have to remember how large the families were in those day. But forget the size of the family for a few minutes and just work on a small luncheon. Even if the hostess was only having half a dozen guests that means six times four which was a small number of pieces in the luncheon set. Add a couple

of large centerpieces, a couple of oval doilies, a set for the hostess, and you have over thirty pieces. Large families would have required twice that number or more.

Unlike the centerpiece, the doily was named for a living person, a Mr. Doily (no given name has been found so far) who was a seventeenth century English merchant and draper. His name has also been found spelled Doyley. According to the records he made quite a name for himself selling fine fabrics and dry goods. It is believed the doilies were made and used as needed during the balance of the seventeenth and eighteenth centuries, but it would be well into the nineteenth century before women would begin making doilies in record numbers and more or less according to some kind of standard measurements. And those measurements are one of the things that can help in determining whether the piece is a doily or centerpiece. Even they are not infallible, as it is still next to impossible to determine if a 12-inch piece was made originally to be used as a centerpiece or a doily. In many cases collectors have given up trying to determine their original uses and just use them to fit their own needs.

Although knowing the measurements used to make the centerpieces and doilies helps, it isn't foolproof. We all had some strong-willed grandmothers who didn't mind one bit breaking the rules. Some felt their rules were better and more realistic than any that were published in a book or magazine. Generally, doilies were only used when tablecloths were not which meant the table was practically covered in doilies. It had to be to accommodate the place setting as well as all the serving pieces. Try to picture these beautiful handmade doilies filled with Haviland china, sterling silver flatware, cutglass stemmed ware, and assorted serving dishes on a long mahogany dining room table. It must have been an elegant sight indeed. Perhaps that helps to explain why there are so many collectors of household linens today; they want to retain some of the elegance of the past.

Admittedly the 12-inch controversial doily could be used as either a centerpiece or a doily, it was generally recognized as the service plate doily. Equally acceptable was the five-inch tumbler or goblet doily. In those days the beverage pitcher, usually a cut glass one for fine dining, was kept on the table. It had its own doily, a ten-inch one unless the pitcher required a different size. Coffee or tea was served at most meals which meant the coffee urn might be on the sideboard but a doily was needed for the cup and saucer, or both. We were unable to find measurements for a saucer doily but it was established that a four-inch size was suitable for a cup. It is possible the old custom of saucering one's coffee or tea is responsible. Early on beautiful flint glass cup plates were used for the cup while the beverage cooled in the deep saucer. It is just possible the doilies were made to be used under the cup plates, and then later under the cups. Three more doilies, all the same seven-inch size, were included in the formal place setting sets. One was for the bullion, one for the frappé, and the third

for the finger bowl. A bread and butter plate was also part of the place setting and it required an eight-inch doily. Carafes were also used on the table and they might require either a nine or eleven-inch doily depending on the size of the base. Bread was still considered one of the essential foods so it was served at each meal. This meant there had to be a bread tray, often a cutglass one. The recommended size was eleven by sixteen inches.

Foods like olives and celery might not be served at every meal, but you can rest assured the perfect housewife had doilies for both dishes. The generally accepted size for the celery dish was nine by fifteen inches while the olive dish required a round doily, ten inches in diameter. There was hardly a family in America that didn't have a rose garden. Roses were the favorite flower to grow and to cut and if they had roses, to be socially correct, they had to have a number of rose bowls. These might be pattern glass, cutglass, or art glass. And if they had rose bowls, they had doilies for them. The accepted size was nine inches.

All of the information about doilies has been gleaned from various and sundry "ladies and needlecraft" magazines dating from around 1900 to 1925. These magazines can be found in many antiques shops and malls priced around $2 to $10 each. If you want to learn more about your household linens, they are an excellent source.

Set of doilies, one for each place setting. Large one was referred to as a centerpiece. $20-$25 for each place setting.

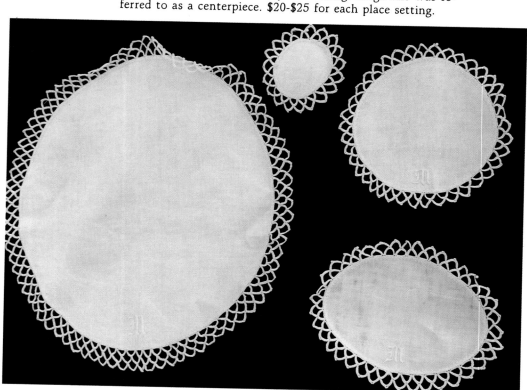

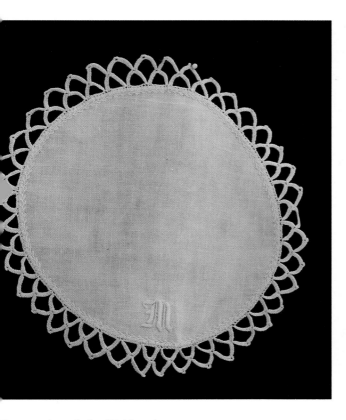

Service plate doily. $7-$9 each.

Tumbler doily from that set. All pieces had featherstitching around the edge of the fabric, monogrammed letter M, and open crocheted lace around the edge. $5-$6.

Knitted doily for rose bowl. $15-$18.

Knitted doily with old knitting needles used to make it. $17-$20.

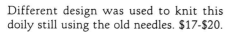

Different design was used to knit this doily still using the old needles. $17-$20.

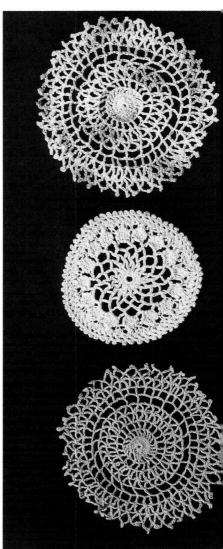

Three tumbler doilies crocheted in threads of different color. $4-$7 each.

Tatted doily. $7-$9.

Crocheted doily perfect for silver candleholder. $11-$14.

Crocheted doily large enough to be used as a centerpiece. $12-$16.

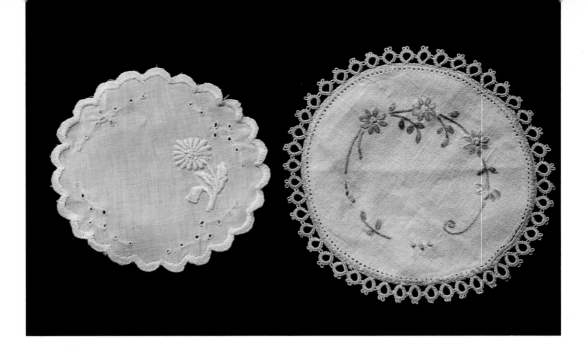

Small, white, embroidered tumbler doily. $5-$7. Larger doily is embroidered and has blue tatted lace edging. $8-$10.

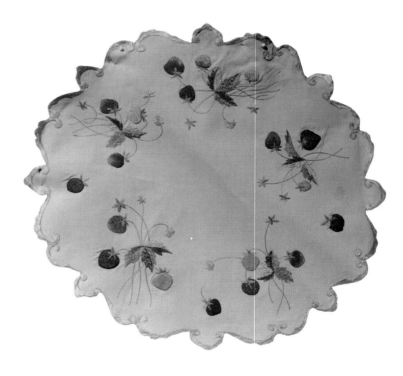

Strawberries embroidered in silk thread decorate this doily. $15-$18.

Two place mats or doilies from a set of six. Set also included a table runner. $30-$40 for the complete set.

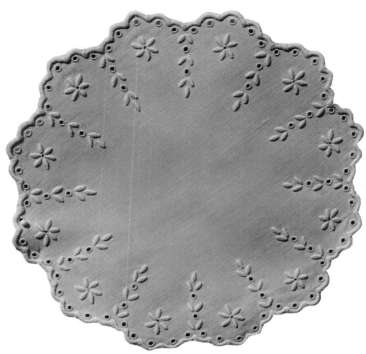

White linen doily heavily embroidered in white. $15-$19.

Late Battenberg lace doily. $10-$12.

Heavy colored embroidery on beige linen. $18-$24.

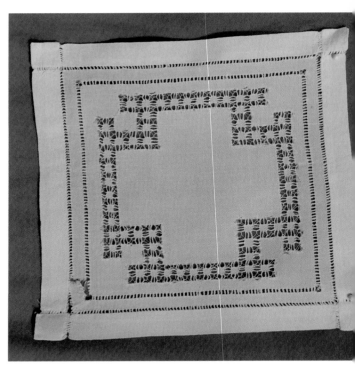

Old drawn work doilies are very fragile. Many damaged pieces can be repaired, but should be purchased at bargain prices. $4-$5.

Two white-on-white doilies. $7-$9 each.

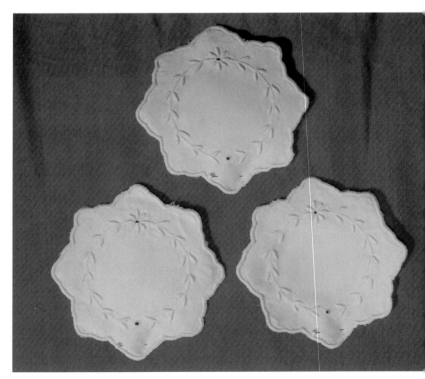

Half of a set of six tumbler doilies. $15-$20 for the set.

Two, small white-on-white doilies. $6-$9 each.

White-on-white oblong doily was probably made to be used
under a celery dish or bread tray. $9-$12. Crocheted doily
could have been used for several purposes. $6-$8.

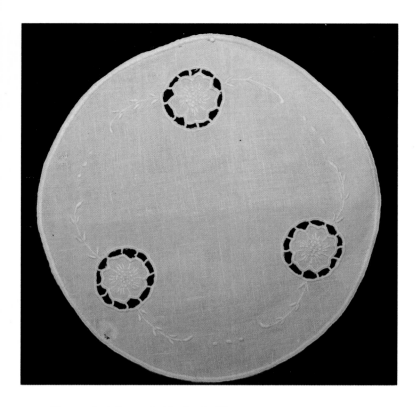

Cutwork doily probably for bullion cup.
$7-$9.

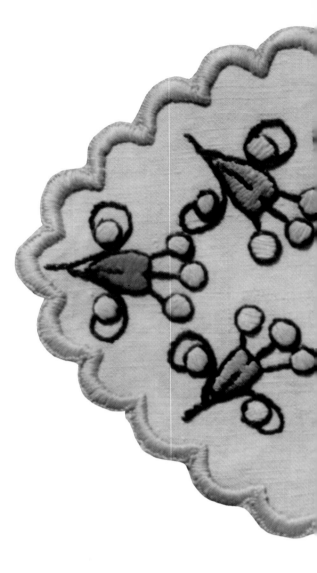

Heavy, colorful embroidery covers this
doily. $15-$18.

Lovely old Battenberg lace doily with
embroidered linen center. $20-$25.

Square doily with only one row of drawn
work. $5-$7.

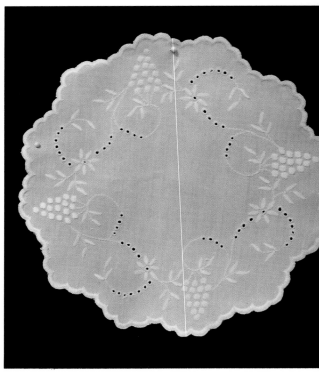

Doily with embroidered grape design. $9-$12.

Doily made of drawn work with crocheted lace edging. $12-$17.

Oblong doily done in Hardanger embroidery. Not the best workmanship hence the low price. $8-$10.

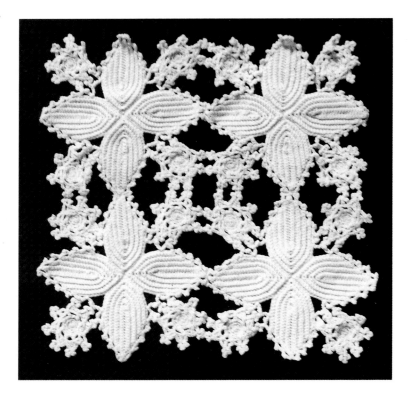

Crocheted doily. $9-$15.

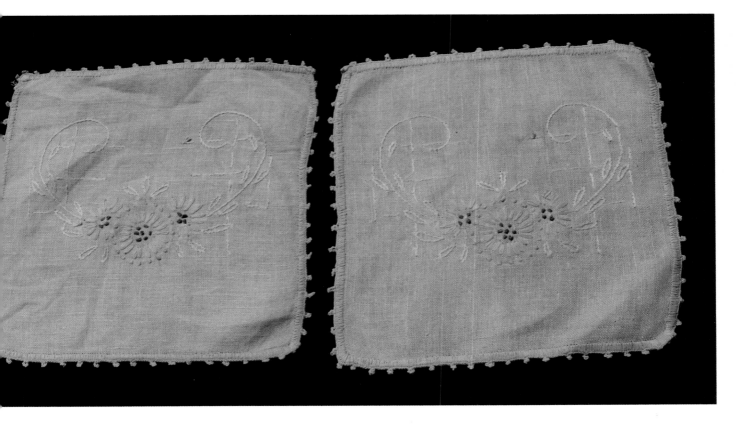

Two embroidered linen doilies. $7-$9 each.

Crocheted doily probably for a rose bowl.
$11-$15.

Crocheted flowers form the center and
edging for this doily. $15-$18.

Small, square linen doily covered with drawn work. $12-$15.

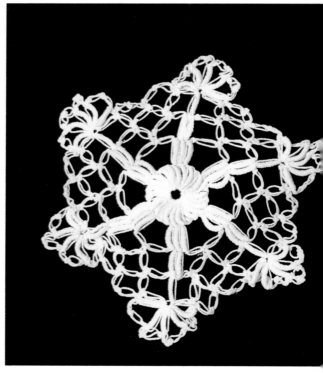

Fabric doily with feather stitching around the hem. Crocheted edging. $8-10.

Different crochet stitches were used to make this yellow and white doily. $8-$10.

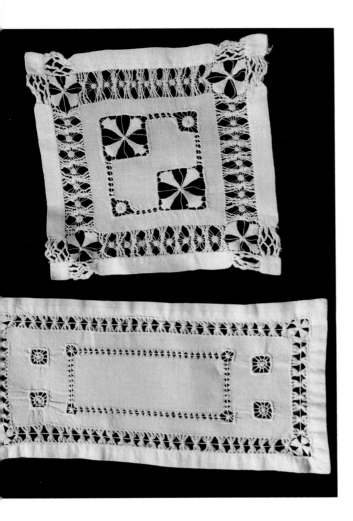

Doilies were made for special occasions like this holly decorated one for Christmas. $13-$17.

Drawn work doilies. $9-$15 each.

Embroidered bread tray doily edged with lace. $9-$12.

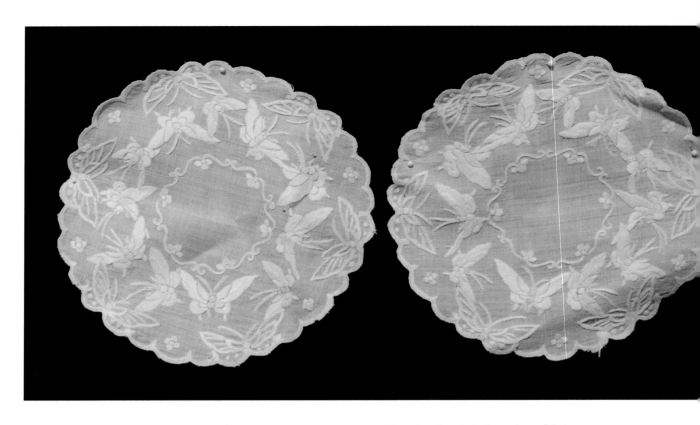

Pair of embroidered doilies, sheer fabric, butterfly design. $15-$20 pair.

Doily with embroidered waterlilies and cutwork. $9-$12.

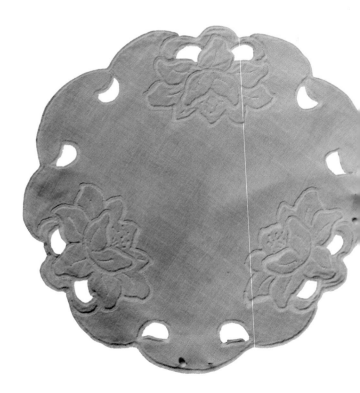

Silk doily with embroidery and drawn work. $9-$15.

Heavy silk embroidery on net doily. $23-$28.

Crocheted doily. $11-$15.

Heavily embroidered doily with factory-made lace. $12-$17.

Unusual shape for bread tray doily. $12-$17.

Two embroidered doilies. $9-$11 each.

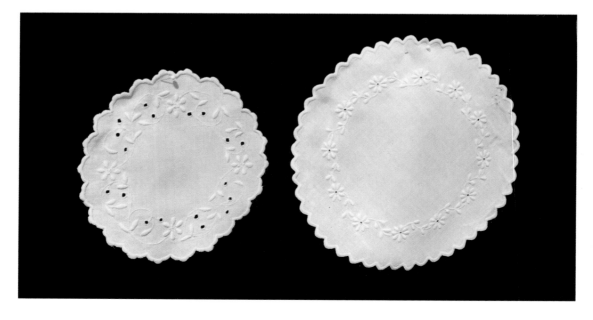

Embroidered tumbler doily (left), larger doily. $9-$11 each.

Doily crocheted in red. Unusual. $18-$23.

Embroidered doily, part of a set. $9-$12.

Hairpin lace and crochet decorate this linen doily. $15-$19.

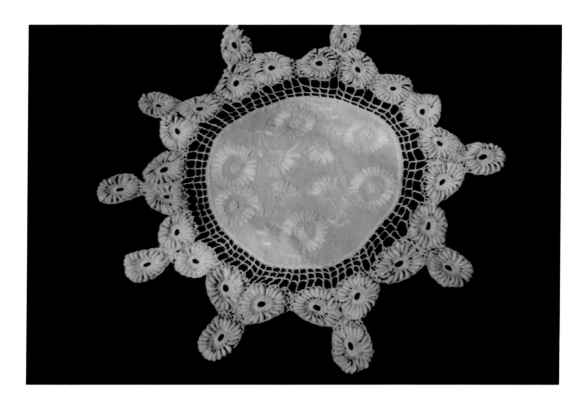

Large doily, embroidered flowers in center, trimmed with crocheted lace. $18-$23.

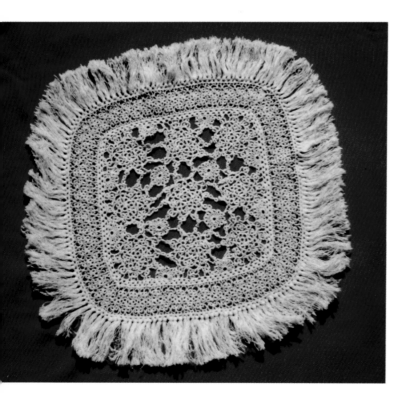

Doily made with a combination of tatting and crochet. Heavy fringe around the edge. $15-$20.

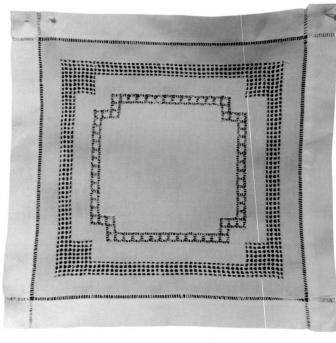

Doily with different drawn work in different design. $10-$14.

This is one of the old embroidered cloths that was used behind the kitchen sink to protect the wall. $20-$25.

An envelope type storage bag. Purpose unknown. $15-$18.

Lavishly embroidered storage bag. $20-$27.

Storage bag done in red embroidery. $17-$24.

Corner of the cover for the hot roll basket. $10-$12.

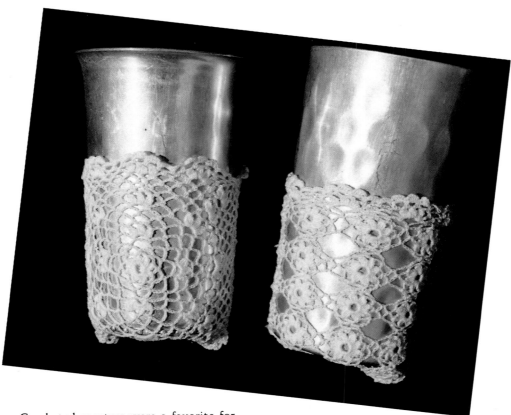

Crocheted coasters were a favorite for
tumblers holding cold summer beverages.
Six for $12.

Heavier thread was used to crochet these
coasters. Six for $10-$12.

Only the person who crocheted this butterfly knew how it was going to be used.
$10-$12.

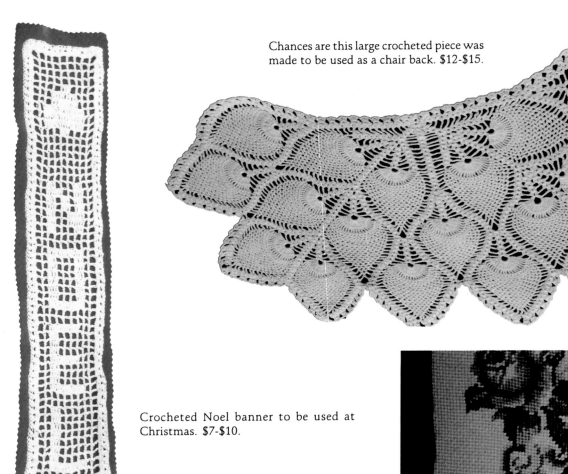

Chances are this large crocheted piece was made to be used as a chair back. $12-$15.

Crocheted Noel banner to be used at Christmas. $7-$10.

Hooked chair seat, eagle design. $15-$18.

Bell pull done in petit point and needle-point. $25-$30.

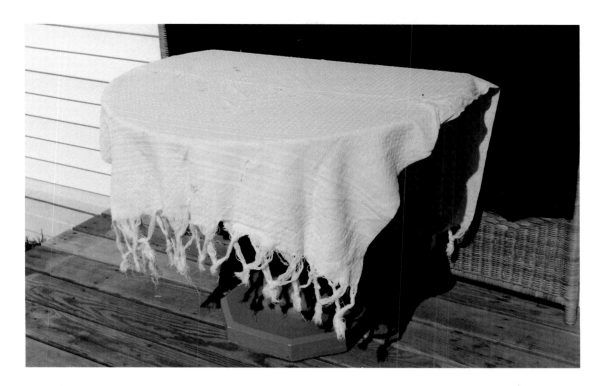

Use for this small bedspread piece with fringe on either end is unknown. $8-$10.

Scotties were so popular in the forties and fifties, burlap came stamped ready for hooking. $5-$10.

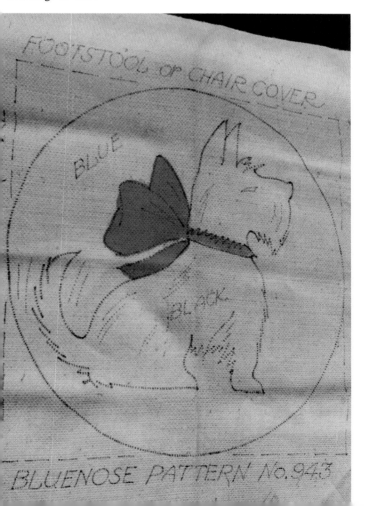

This album cover appears to have been made from scratch. $18-$23.

Embroidered cloth done in maker's native language. $13-$17.

Could be crocheted shelf cloths or chair backs. $7-$9 each.

Embroidered laundry bag. $9-$12.

Stamped clock faces along with unassembled cases were offered in many needlework magazines during the sixties. $35-
$40.

Package of hot iron transfers of butterflies and flowers. $3-$5.

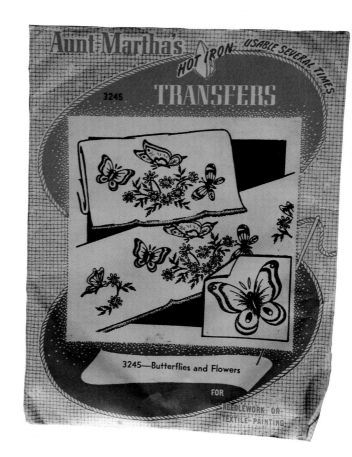

From around 1920 on to the sixties, hot iron transfers (to stamp your own pieces for embroidery) were offered for sale in dime stores, craft shops, and in most needlecraft magazines. Since they had to be discarded after they were used, the old ones are not plentiful now. $3-$5.

Animals were another favorite with needleworkers. $3-$5.

Albums like this were probably sold as kits with the buyer doing all the needlework. $25-$35.

Later, embroidered bed linens were as important to the ladies as feather beds had been earlier. Rose designs were very popular for bed linens. $3-$5.

Someone probably knitted this small replica of the flag to hang outside on the Fourth of July. $35-$45.

Many small white luncheon and bridge cloths had matching crocheted corners on both the cloths and the napkins. Four napkins $14-$16.

Chapter 10
Napkins and Napkin Rings

The popularity of fabric napkins has waxed and waned through the centuries. At present their popularity is well below average. Several factors have contributed to this situation. One is the fact so few people actually dine anymore; they generally eat on the run. Then there is the case of the working homemaker. She simply does not have time to launder piles of fabric napkins. Today paper napkins can serve the same purpose, not as elegantly perhaps, but they serve somewhat the same need, and with a lot less work. And without a napkin to hold, the napkin ring went the way of all unnecessary things: it was packed away until it was discovered again, and then it was brought out and honored as a collectible or antique, depending on its age. Since fine fabric napkins were so much a part of the gracious dining enjoyed by our parents and grandparents, we have to save the old napkins if we are going to save the old tablecloths. They were usually made in matching sets, that is, a tablecloth might have anywhere from four to twelve matching napkins depending on the size of the tablecloth. The sizes of the napkin could vary from about 8 inches to as much as 24 inches. All of the fine ones, like the tablecloths, were hemmed by hand using tiny little stitches. Many of the napkins as well as the tablecloths have lots of needlework designs either crocheted, tatted, or embroidered.

In the very early days napkins did not match the tablecloths, in fact, in some instances in the Middle Ages the tablecloths were not even mentioned while the use of the napkins is well documented. The lavish feast of the ancient Romans was served to guests who reclined on couches to eat their meals. Napkins were used to catch the food that spilled as well as to wipe their hands and mouth.

They didn't have forks in those days so eating with only a knife and perhaps a spoon could be a bit messy. It is interesting that at those meals or feasts the host might furnish the napkins for his guests, or the guest might bring his own. No doubt this was decided when the invitation was issued. Of course the guest list was not really that large as only the very affluent which included those of royal blood, the very rich, and the clergy from the well established churches, those attended by the rich and the royals, were included. Records show that by the end of the 16th century the place setting of the royals consisted of a knife, spoon, and a napkin. The napkin must have been extremely large as it was used to cover the ruff, those multiple ruffles the royals were wearing around their necks at the time. The ruffs were easily soiled and unbelievably hard to wash and iron; therefore the wearer was very careful not to soil it if it was at all possible. Soiling could be prevented provided the wearer was careful to tie a napkin over the ruff and under the chin. The napkin had to be large enough for the ends to tie in the back. If it wasn't, there was a problem that created an old saying "to make ends meets" that persists today.

The role of the napkin diminished somewhat in the late 17th century when the fork became a part of dining. Now people, and especially guests, could spear their food rather than eat it with their fingers or from a knife. This lessened the spills and the greasy mouth and fingers. The napkins also became smaller. Since they could now be placed on the table, their appearance became important. This in turn created the need for folding them in order to show off their handiwork as by this time they were being decorated with all types of needlework.

Fringed napkins with embroidery. Six $12-$14.

Reports are napkin folders were hired for special feasts, and the best ones knew at least twenty-five different ways to fold napkins. Today it is suggested that when one uses old fabric napkins, they should be folded twice to form a square with the decorated corner outside. It should then be placed on the left side of the place setting. Antiquers have always had a mind of their own, and once they have collected the items they want, they may want to use them as they were used originally, or they may just simply want to display them. For that reason you may or may not see lots of tables set with old fabric napkins in napkin rings.

Custom had not changed that much when the Puritans settled in America. In Mary Caroline Crawford's book *Social Life In Old New England* published in 1914, she poses the question, "Would we be shocked if a guest pulled a knife from his pocket, cut his meat, and then ate with his fingers?" She assumed they ate that way and felt the old saying "fingers were made before forks" originated with them. She goes on to describe some of the etiquette rules found in a small book written by a Boston schoolmaster named Eleazar Moody. We know they used napkins then because one of Moody's rules

was "Foul not the napkin all over, but at one corner only."

American women have always made and used the most beautiful of table linens, but if we had to pick a time when we thought they were the best and the most plentiful, it would certainly be around the turn of the present century. And it lasted for decades. This was a time when women didn't work outside the home, yet they were still living on the edge of that era where their ancestors insisted "Idle hands are the devil's workshop," so they not only kept busy, but insisted their daughters do the same. Needlework was a very acceptable chore. Not only did it keep the women and girls busy, but they could create lovely things for their homes.

The Victorian era can also be classified as the era of gracious living. It was a time when everything was done correctly, maybe a little overdone in some cases, but always according to the current rules of etiquette. There can be no question this was the time when household linens reached their peak, both in making and in use. Napkin rings, especially sterling silver and silver plated ones, were very popular then. Every home is believed to have had enough for each place setting, no matter how large the family or the table. So we have to wonder why so many handmade napkins rings can be found today. Were they made to be used while they saved the silver ones, or maybe the family could not afford the silver, and the housewife made the crocheted, tatted, and embroidered napkin rings because she needed them? We will probably never know, but we do know that exquisite sets of handmade napkin rings can still be found—and at prices that seem quite reasonable.

The price of napkins may be rising soon, and the quantity becoming scarce, if an idea we heard about recently catches on. Admittedly, the price of ordinary napkins has been very low for several years. Now a few collectors are taking advantage of that to make duvets out of the napkins. Depending on the size of the napkins and the size duvet one wants, about twelve to twenty napkins will be required—for the top. The same number will be required if the bottom is also made of napkins. Some of the makers are using large, matching table cloths to make the bottom of the duvet. One duvet maker is really making a lavish one using fancy monogrammed napkins, and working them into a design. The napkins with pretty embroidered, floral designs could also be worked into an elegant duvet. Another collector makes beautiful decorator pillows out of napkins.

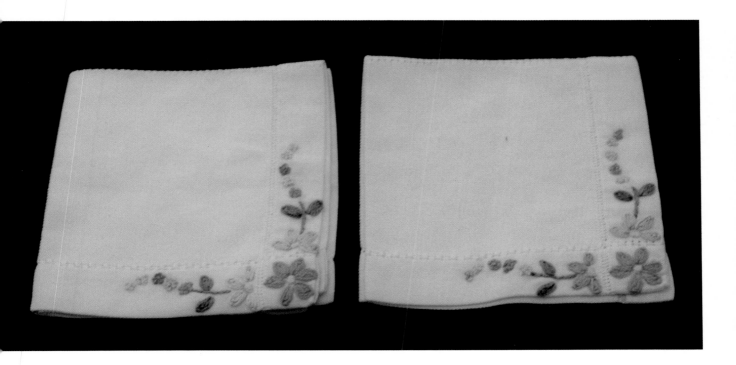

Napkins and napkin rings were made in a variety of styles, shapes, and materials. These napkins are a bit unusual in that they are embroidered on the wide hem. Six $15-$18.

Two of a set of six heavily embroidered napkins. $18-$24 for the set.

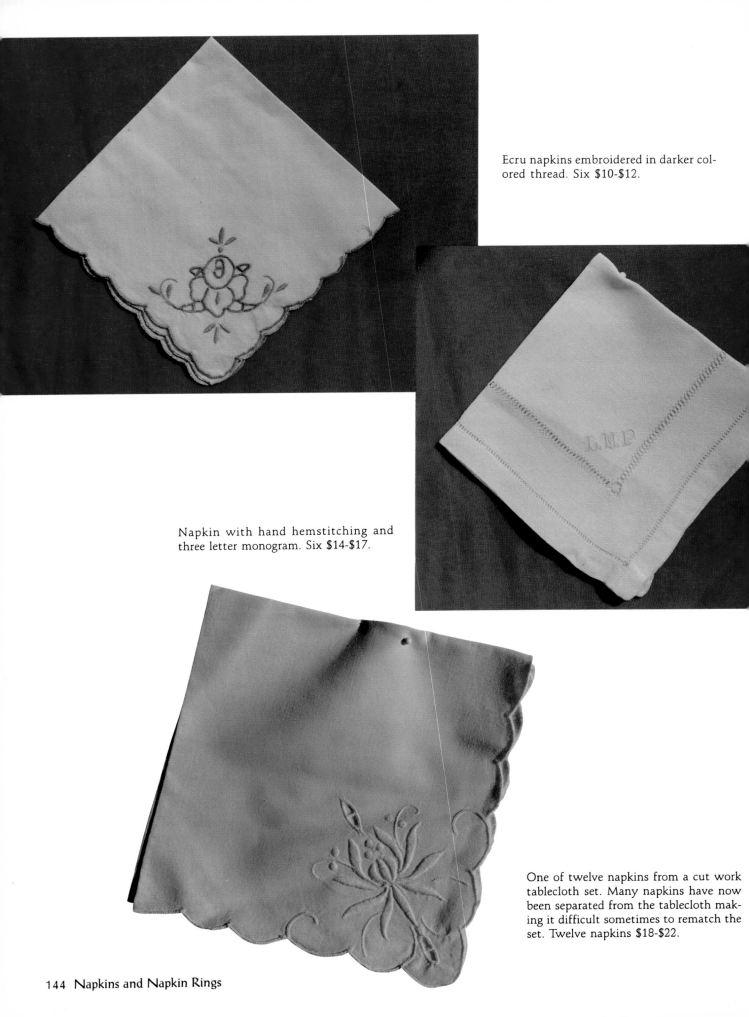

Ecru napkins embroidered in darker colored thread. Six $10-$12.

Napkin with hand hemstitching and three letter monogram. Six $14-$17.

One of twelve napkins from a cut work tablecloth set. Many napkins have now been separated from the tablecloth making it difficult sometimes to rematch the set. Twelve napkins $18-$22.

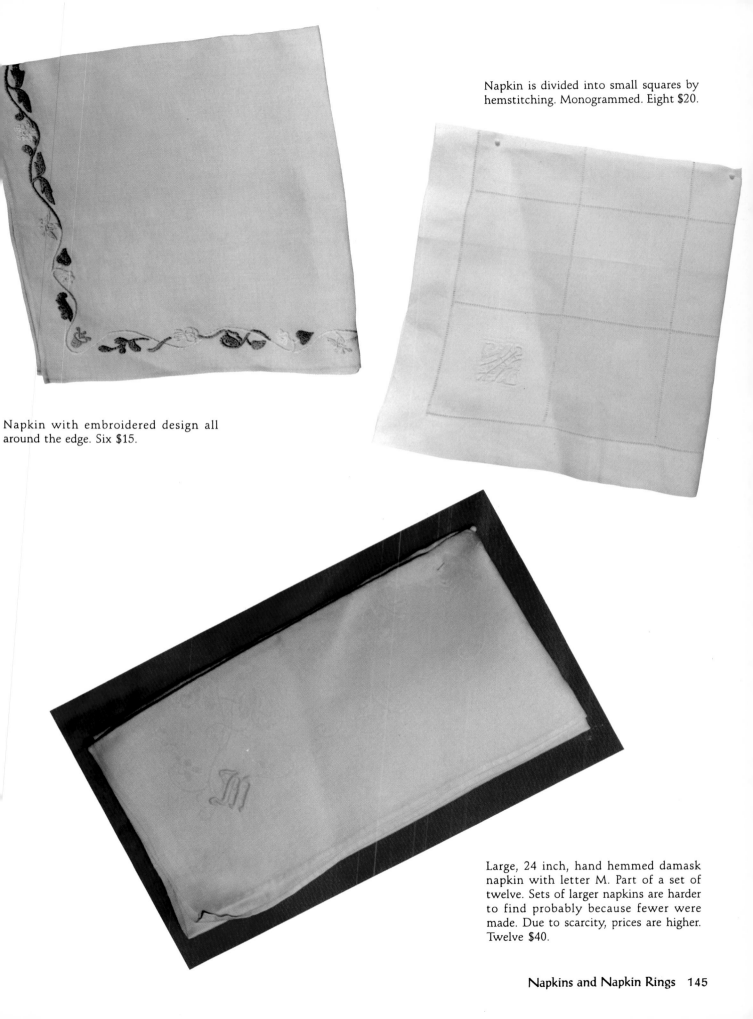

Napkin is divided into small squares by hemstitching. Monogrammed. Eight $20.

Napkin with embroidered design all around the edge. Six $15.

Large, 24 inch, hand hemmed damask napkin with letter M. Part of a set of twelve. Sets of larger napkins are harder to find probably because fewer were made. Due to scarcity, prices are higher. Twelve $40.

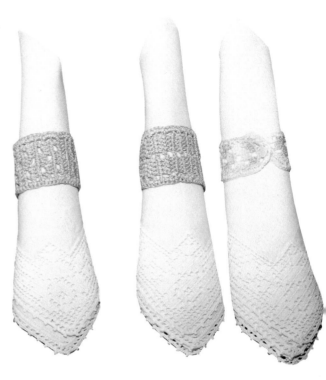

Fine linen napkin with F monogram. Six
$15-$18.

Crocheted napkin rings on napkins.

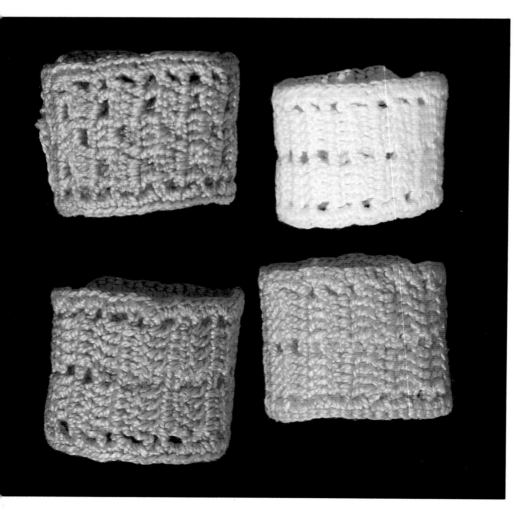

Napkin rings were so important women
who could not afford to buy them, made
their own. Set of four crocheted rings $10-
$15.

Heavily embroidered, linen napkin ring with tiny button and button hole. This single ring was found in a box of small oddities at an estate sale. No matching rings have ever been found. $7-$9.

Two of a set of six tatted napkin rings. Shown with the embroidered one above. Six tatted rings $25-$30.

Native Americans in the Northeast made all kinds of souvenirs to sell to the summer tourists. One of the novelties was a birchbark napkin ring decorated with real porcupine quills. Six $50-$60.

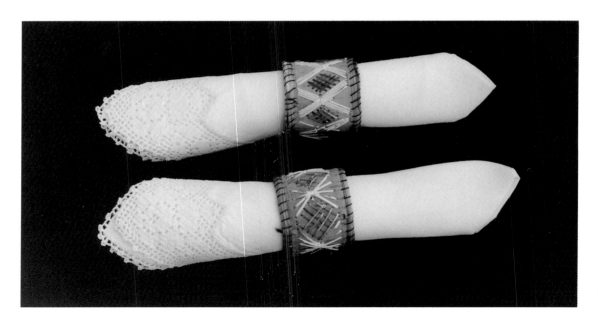

Native American-made, birch bark napkin rings with fancier porcupine quill design. Six $50-$60.

Hand carved, wooden napkin rings decorated with African animals. Made in Kenya. Six $50-$60.

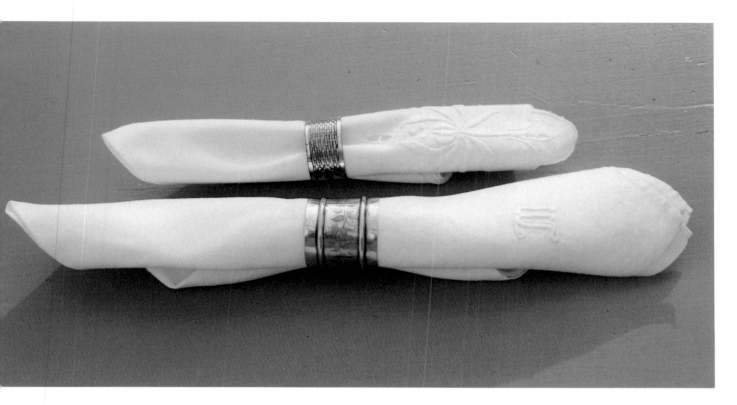

Two different types of silver plated napkin rings. Wide one $7-$9. Narrow one. $5-$8.

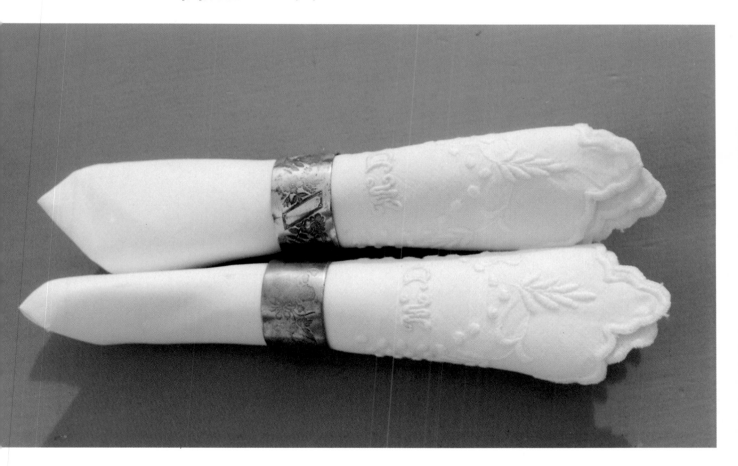

Two silver plated napkin rings. $9-$15 each.

Less than one fourth of an old woven coverlet was purchased
for $1. Part of it was used to make this lamp shade.

Chapter 11
Uses for Damaged Linens

It is difficult for people who have or are doing needlework to discard an old piece even though it is damaged. They immediately start searching for a way to salvage the good parts. Some even try to devise ways to make it usable again. It seems this was practiced more by the early makers than now, and that is easily understandable as they knew exactly how much work had gone into the making of each piece. A centerpiece found recently shows how they covered a hole that could have been burned or torn in the center. A small doily with a similar design was sewn over the hole. It would have been much better if the repairer had cut the fabric close under the doily and whipped it around the edges. It would have made it look like an original job rather than a patch job.

Most damaged pieces can be bought in our area for prices like $1 to $2 for small pieces, and up to $5 to $10 for damaged woven or embroidered bedspreads, or loom woven coverlets. There is enough good material in the large pieces to make a number of things. In fact, the stuffed sea lion, a pillow, and several lamp shades were made out of the good parts of half a loom woven blue and white coverlet. The blue and white shades are very attractive on old milk glass oil lamps. Actually lamp shades made of damaged linens are the most challenging (trying to make the fabric and the designs fit) and the most rewarding as they are so pretty, different, and useful. The flint glass lamp has a shade made using the design on either end of a dresser scarf. The middle which had suffered quite a bit of damage still had

enough good linen to make the sides as it was a long scarf. Sometimes there isn't enough fabric left to make the sides. In that case find a damaged piece made of identical fabric and use it for the sides. Lace tablecloths also make lamp shades that are most attractive on all old lamps. Or you may get lucky and find a few yards of fine old lace that is just right for lamp shade making. Both sides of an embroidered pillow top were used to make a shade for lamp made by wiring a stoneware jug.

If you have grandchildren or are interested in dolls, damaged linens make excellent bedspreads for doll beds and carriages. Usually a quarter of a small tablecloth makes a good size bedspread. The one in the illustration looks much too large, because the mattress was missing. It fits better with a mattress. The ends of some scarves make great doll bed spreads while the smaller ones make excellent doll carriage robes.

We have recently been experimenting with round tablecloths. They make a "different, one-of-a-kind" valance for windows. The window may be left open or blinds can be used. The tablecloth has to fit the window so it may take some comparison shopping to get the right size for your windows. And then you may not be able to find matching ones for all the windows in a room. In that case you may have to mix and match, which also makes an interesting room. We haven't even scratched the surface when it comes to making useful things out of damaged linens, as more and more appear on the market each year.

A yard of fine old factory made lace priced $7 made this lamp shade and several others.

After a hole developed in this centerpiece, someone took the handmade lace off to use on something else. Ordinarily that would make it useless, but a small group of needleworkers who know how much work went into these pieces have begun finding uses for them, sort of a recycling process. Damaged pieces usually sell in the $1 to $3 range.

Close-up of the embroidered butterflies that can be used on a lamp shade, or cut out and sewn on an outside pocket on a blouse or skirt. They can also be used to cover a worn or damaged place on a dress.

The balance of the piece of woven coverlet was used to make this shade for an old iron floor lamp.

The font of this late oil lamp was filled with bright colored, artificial flowers, and the shade was made with scraps from a badly damaged lace tablecloth.

This lamp shade was made from some badly worn church vestments.

Piano scarves are larger than other scarves which makes them ideal for large lampshades.

No matter how badly damaged lace tablecloths are, there is usually more than enough for a large lampshade or two.

Large shade on cut glass lamp.

When one end of a scarf is badly damaged but the other is good, it can be used to make a bedspread for a doll bed or a cloth for a clock shelf.

This is an example of how two damaged pieces may be needed to make a lampshade. The middle of one dresser scarf was in shreds, but the embroidered ends were perfect. So the two embroidered ends were used on either side of the shade while matching linen from a scarf with reverse damage was used for the sides.

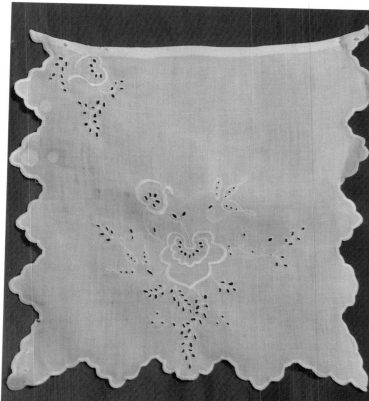

Both sides of a gaily embroidered pillow was used to make this shade. Matching linen from another piece was used on the sides. The dirty pillow top was bought at a yard sale for 25 cents and laundered.

Damaged dresser scarf was used to make this shade.

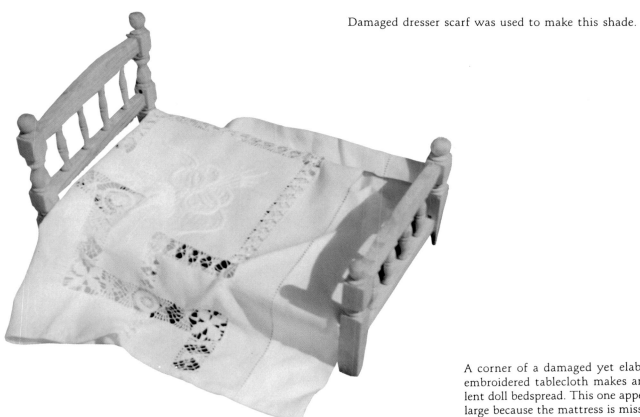

A corner of a damaged yet elaborately embroidered tablecloth makes an excellent doll bedspread. This one appears too large because the mattress is missing.

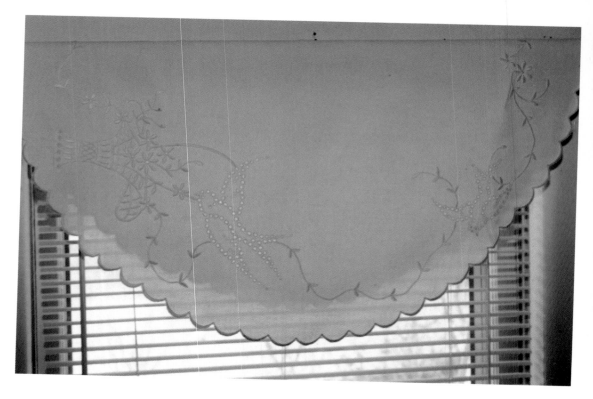

Round embroidered tablecloths make excellent and unusual valances for windows.

Toy or pillow made out of damaged woven coverlets.

Pillow made from damaged bedspread.

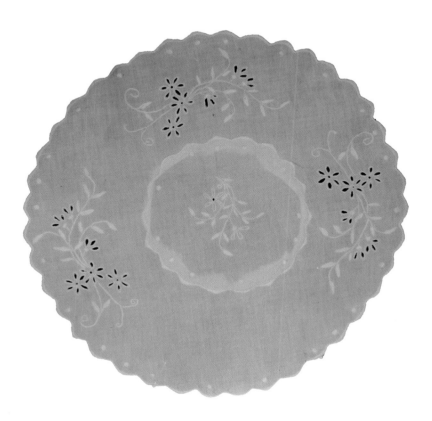

Doilies can be useful in repairing centerpieces that have holes
in the center. This one could have been trimmed closer to
make it blend in.

Chapter 12
Caring for Old Linens

Today there is some controversy surrounding the care and cleaning of old linens. Some collectors lean toward leaving the linens yellowed, as found, while others insist they need to be laundered. The first group seems to think the yellowing of the linens is like the patina of fine furniture—it is an authentic sign of age. On the other side is another group that remembers the snowy white linens made and used by their grandmothers and great grandmothers, and they are determined to return every piece to its former whiteness. After hearing the arguments of both sides, we feel that each has a good point which leaves us with the thought that the saying "to each his own" was never more appropriate.

The first group doesn't use their linens like the latter group, in fact, the majority uses them sparingly. They believe more dirt, moisture, and sunlight are very harmful to old fabrics, and for that reason only vacuum them now and then. When they do vacuum they use a piece of cheese cloth over the nozzle to protect the fabric. Even this can break weakened threads they think, and this is probably true of the really old linens, but the chance of the average collector finding many of those pieces is remote. When found the price of those pieces can be extremely high. So for that reason we agree with the latter group who uses their old linens and launders them on a more or less regular basis. Linens were made to be used and enjoyed.

All the "ladies and needlecraft" magazines published around 1900 to 1925 carried instructions for caring for linens. Of course they were describing ways to launder the new linens which could stand stronger soaps and cleaners than the older ones we have now. Regardless of which magazine all those old instructions seem to have one thing in common—always use warm water and a mild soap to wash linens. That still applies today. They also recommended spreading the linens with yellow spots on the grass to dry as they said that would help eliminate the yellow.

They also offered much advice on ironing. One had to be more careful with pieces embroidered with silk thread than those done in cotton. The steam from the hot iron on the damp linen would harm the silk thread, they said. Embroidered pieces should be ironed first on the top then on the reverse side as that made the embroidery stand out more. Ironing and folding pieces the same way repeatedly could cause the threads to break more easily on the folds; therefore collectors should change the way they fold their linens each time they are laundered. If the bridge cloth has been folded in the middle and then folded again to quarter it, next time make three folds instead of two. And on big pieces like bedspreads and tablecloths, don't fold them when you are storing them. Roll them up instead.

Collecting More Household Linens will cover factory-made fabrics, needlework pictures, pillowcases, shams and bolsters, quilts and coverlets, rugs, scarfs and runners, sheets and blankets, tablecloths, towels and splashers, and tea cart cloths. There will also be more information on using and caring for old and damaged linens.

Embroidered centerpiece with butterfly design. $8-11.

Crocheted red and white centerpiece. $9-12.

Round, linen centerpiece embroidered in colors. $7-10.

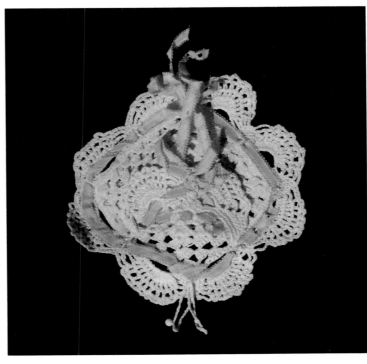

Victorians loved ribbon and used it on much of their needle-work. This crocheted watch holder was laced with pink rib-bon. Due to the rarity it is expensive. $25-30.

Square crocheted doily laced with pink ribbon. $8-11.

Large crocheted piece with peacock design. Could be used as a pillow top or framed for picture. $20-25.

Battenberg lace doily. $15-20.